FOR EXPOSURE

The Life and Times of a Small Press Publisher

JASON SIZEMORE

www.apexbookcompany.com

FOR EXPOSURE

The Life and Times of a Small Press Publisher

JASON SIZEMORE

An Apex Publications Book
Lexington, Kentucky

For Exposure: The Life and Times of a Small Press Publisher

TPB ISBN: 978-1937009-30-4
Hardcover ISBN: 978-193-7009-31-1

Cover art and jacket design © by Justin Stewart
Typography by Maggie Slater

Published by Apex Publications, LLC
PO Box 24323
Lexington, KY 40524

Printed in the United States of America

First Edition

www.apexbookcompany.com

For all the minions,
your generosity has been
EXPOSED.

Table of Contents

Prologue: See the Child — 1

Chapter One: The Risk Master — 9

Chapter Two: The Ham — 19

Chapter Three: A Forgotten Night — 29

A Forgotten Night: Eyewitness Rebuttal by Justin Stewart — 40

Chapter Four: Legends of the Slush Pile — 43

Chapter Five: Death by a Thousand Cuts — 53

Chapter Six: Another Forgotten Night, With Fact Checking by Maurice Broaddus — 61

Chapter Seven: Business Acumen — 71

Chapter Eight: Building the Legend of Apex — 85

Building the Legend of Apex: Eyewitness Rebuttal by Elaine Blose — 96

Building the Legend of Apex: Eyewitness Rebuttal by Geoffrey Girard — 101

Chapter Nine: Stoned and Delirious — 105

Stoned and Delirious: Eyewitness Rebuttal by Sara M. Harvey — 116

Chapter Ten: Waterfalls — 123

The Case of the Mysterious Warm Splatters: Eyewitness Rebuttal by Monica Valentinelli — 137

Chapter Eleven: For Exposure — 147

For Exposure: Eyewitness Rebuttal by Lesley Conner — 153

Chapter Twelve: Lord Hugo—159

Lord Hugo: Eyewitness Rebuttal by Janet Harriett — 165

Chapter Thirteen: Parting Shot — 169

1. "Faithful Reader" by Jettie Necole — 170

2. "Unless…"by Maggie Slater — 173

3. "I Remember the Future of Apex Publications"
by Michael A. Burstein — 179

4. "Feed the Beast" by Jaym Gates — 181

Acknowledgements — 182

Biographies — 183

See the child cower behind the pew. He's a matchstick of a kid, pale with a ball of thick, curly red hair towering outward like a healthy flame. At the age of ten, his imagination is an uncontrollable beast, running wild with visions of the demonic afflictions that affect the men and women jerking about on the worn brown carpet of Big Creek Baptist Church.

These are people he knows, people he's known his entire life. They're a serious lot, not the sort to just fall to the ground and yell out unknown words and incantations. Speaking in tongues, as the old-timers call it. Ethel Bowling, a sweet elderly woman who teaches his Sunday school class, yells and cries out for the Lord while lying in a fetal position by his feet. Only 45 minutes earlier, she had rubbed the child's hair and given him a dry kiss on his left cheek.

"Such beautiful hair this one has," she'd said. "Did'ya get it from your momma's side?" It's a common refrain he hears, particularly from the older folks. No Sizemore in memory has ever had red hair, and members of the small community never fail to note the aberration.

The child does not understand what is wrong with the adults. Well, that's not *quite* right. He reckons they've been touched by the Holy Spirit. But why should the Holy Spirit, a benign and powerful extension of God, see fit to put a person into conniptions and tears? Preacher Hayes, a bent figure in an old-fashioned grey cotton suit and tie, stands at the front of the church, sweating profusely, holding his cracked and wrinkled Bible skyward while he punctuates every refrain of "Amazing Grace" being sung by the choir on a raised dais with a bellowing "Praise the Lord!"

The whole setting—the crying, the speaking in tongues, the loud preaching—frightens the child.

Preacher Hayes says the only way to avoid eternal hell and damnation, to avoid suffering for a thousand years in the Lake of Fire, is to accept Christ as your salvation and to be baptized in the name of the Lord Jesus.

The child comes out from behind the pew and steps over his Sunday school teacher. He walks toward the preacher.

I dig into ancient Sizemore history to build a foundation for how I came to be a geek, not to belittle the religious beliefs held by members of Big Creek Baptist Church. Most of the congregation were true men and women of Christian faith. At the time, I was a true believer, and because of that I was instilled with a sense of wonder and fear by stories and incidents that easily fit into the labels of dark science fiction and horror. I often say that the best book of horror ever written is the Bible.

The church also instilled in me many of what I consider to be my better traits; though as time progresses, I have a habit of shedding them with some regularity.

The most common question I field is, "Sizemore, how did you come about your love and adoration of dark speculative fiction?" The roots dug themselves into the fertile earth of my imagination when I was ten years old. That year, a powerful combination of church, coal mining, a well-meaning grandmother, and my jokester of a mother shaped the public face of the nervous geek who has always lived inside of me.

That's right. I'm here today to cast an accusing finger at my parents and dear ol' grandma.

I had attended church three times a week for the first decade of my life with nary a fear of divine retribution, despite the numerous persuasive tactics employed by good man Preacher Hayes. The old preacher was a real pro. His red-in-the-face, spittle-raining, Bible-pounding, you're-going-to-burn-in-Hell sermons were powerful to behold. In fact, I've spent a lifetime trying to recreate that old man's penetrating, accusatory stare, when he would call out the sinners and would gaze into the eyes of every member of the congregation. I weathered everything the preacher had to offer. On reflection… perhaps my age kept the fear of God out of me.

That changed when my mom decided I had reached an age old enough to join her for Friday horror nights.

One of my mother's most endearing traits is that she's a huge science fiction, fantasy, and horror fan. She was even more so in the 80s. The cheesier the movie, the more enthralling she found it. Nowadays she limits herself to the horrors of the various awful ghost-hunter shows on the SyFy Channel and an occasional cable movie rerun.

Back in 1984, my father was a hard-working coal miner, and Fridays nights were his mandatory overtime shifts. That left Mom alone with me and my little brother Joey. My punk brother would be sent to bed, and she and I would converge in the living room, where movie time would commence.

I handled our first Friday horror nights well enough. Despite being a sheltered and naïve kid, I understood that the inherent silly violence employed in entertaining classics such as *Friday the 13th*, *Pumpkinhead*, and *Halloween* was over the top and fictional. Not that I found the movies silly in a ridiculous manner, but that I recognized them for what they are: films with made-up monsters that terrorized young people who have incredibly poor decision-making skills. Sex kills. And since I was not having sex, I did not fear.

Then one fateful night, Mom rented the double bill of possession: *The Exorcist* and *The Thing*.

Both films frightened the piss out of me.

Those movies (and Mom) created a personal paradigm shift. The way I thought of science fiction and horror changed. The dangers expressed in the plots of those movies suddenly felt more real, more personal.

Both movies deal with possession, one of the spiritual type and the other of the physical. Neither was anything I worried about happening to myself (I figured I had a better chance of being hacked down by a random hillbilly named Jason who lived up some local holler). Furthermore, the gory stuff didn't freak me out like it did other kids. I viewed gore as condiments to enhance the big scares.

Yep, little Jason felt that he was a big boy in big boy movie pants. The two films had scared me, but I had survived. I was totally chill when Mom and I began our usual post-movie analysis—my favorite part of every film night.

"Jason," she asked, "did you enjoy those movies?"

"I did. Way better than the stuff we usually watch. These scared me, especially *The Exorcist*!"

Mom sipped her Jack and Coke and frowned. "Scared you? They better scare you."

What did she mean? Of course I should be scared; they are *horror* movies. Classic horror movies! And *scaring* you is what they're supposed do. The confusion registered on my face and my mom raised an eyebrow. It was her "I'm about to lay the hard truth on a sucker" expression I'd seen way too many times.

"You've been going to church with Granny Sizemore your whole life. Haven't you learned a thing about demonic possession?" She had lit a Virginia Slim cigarette, and it dangled from her mouth like a smoking, ghostly finger.

Of course I knew about possession. It was a favorite topic of Preacher Hayes. I nodded.

"What happened to the girl in *The Exorcist*—little what's-her-name? Reagan?—any of that could happen to me, your brother, your dad. *You.*"

I frowned. The cold creep of fear dripped out of my brain and trickled down my spine. "You" echoed in my head. I shivered. Even the thought of my bratty little brother being possessed by the devil or a demon upset me. "What?" I asked.

"The Bible talks about possession and the casting out of demons. Most preachers and priests you'll talk to will claim to have seen it firsthand, but they won't say much on the matter. I read in *The National Enquirer* once that some Catholic priests

4

are educated in the art of exorcism; there are classes the priests can take at the Vatican."

I thought of the cute little girl Reagan. Head spinning. Projectile green vomit. The embarrassing debasement of a crucifix. "The art of exorcism?" I asked.

Ash dropped from the tip of the cigarette and landed on her nightgown. She brushed it off, leaving a dirty grey smear behind. "You know what else? Aliens are real, too."

I shook my head clear. I needed to kneel to the Lord and pray for my soul immediately. I needed to atone for my sins *right now*. I promised God that I would never have inappropriate thoughts about my fifth grade teacher ever again! I would do anything to keep from being possessed!

And now this, my mother telling me that alien beings are *real*. To be fair, it did occur to me that perhaps she had read too many issues of *The National Enquirer*. But little comfort the thought provided. At that moment, the chilling grip of fear had my brain locked down in panic mode.

"What?" The word seemed to be the only one remaining in my expansive grade-school vocabulary for dealing with all the terrible truths laid about me.

Mom continued. "I've seen aliens. Okay… not aliens, but a UFO. I can't tell you if aliens can possess people, but think about it, if they can make spaceships that fly across the galaxies and land on Earth, then possessing a person shouldn't be such a technological leap. You're a smart kid, Jason; you make the connections."

"When did you see an alien spaceship?" I asked, trying to make the connection.

Mom smiled and took another sip of soda and whiskey. She crushed out the cigarette in a nearby ashtray.

"Me and your daddy were on our way home from Hamilton, Ohio. You were a baby—about six weeks old. Roy was driving. I had you sucking on the teat."

"Ugh, Mom!" Disgust blanketed my fear. The imagery almost brought forth a blast of projectile vomit to rival Reagan's.

"Don't be a prude. I remember the crying tantrums you had when I weaned you off the breast. It took you months to be—"

"*Aliens*, Mom. You and Dad were on the way home." Mom has always loved grossing me out. Sometimes I have to force a redirect to avoid embarrassment and humiliation.

She sighed and her eyes shifted around as she recalled the encounter. "We were on the interstate. The Cincinnati bypass around I-75. It's not a busy road in the middle of a weekday, but nobody was going north or south and we hadn't seen another car in a long time. The day was sunny, a beautiful spring day. That much I remember. You had just taken to nipple when far ahead of us something bright flashed and, just like that, a ship of some sort could be seen lowering itself to the ground in the woods off to our right. It looked like a saucer, just like you see in the papers."

"What papers?"

Mom ignored the question. "After the flash, you started screaming and crying louder than I'd ever heard before. Like you knew something unnatural had happened."

"Maybe the bright light scared me?" I suggested.

"I don't think so. Your face was mashed against my boob with your mouth having at it."

"Yuck, Mom." I course corrected again. "What did you and Dad do?"

"Your father pulled us over to the emergency lane and parked. He took out his big silver revolver from under the seat, the one he takes on long road trips, and tells me he wants to go check on things."

"Did he go?"

"Of course he went. I begged him not to. I cried and screamed right along with you. He paid us no mind. The man is stubborn as a mule. He opened the door to the Nissan, and stepped outside. I watched him push right into the weeds and trees. No less than ten seconds had passed before he runs back inside the car, starts the engine, floors the gas, and threw gravel hauling us the hell out of there."

I felt like Mom was pulling my chain. But at ten years old, I still had a bad habit of believing everything Mom told me as though it was the gospel.

"What did Dad see?"

Mom fished another Virginia Slim from her crumpled pack and lit up. She took a drag and exhaled smoke out of her nose, like a dragon. "He wouldn't tell me. Told me never to ask him about it ever again. So I haven't."

I checked the clock. Dad would be home in about an hour. I totally planned to ask him.

Mom read my intentions. "Don't you dare ask your father about it! He'll be pissed I even told you about the UFO and will get upset thinking about it all."

Somehow, an alien encounter would explain so much about me. The odd personality. The crazy red hair. The social anxiety. The three superpowers.

"Did something happen to us that day?" I asked.

A moment of silence passed. Mom finally said, "I don't know."

It all remains unspoken to this day. What had happened to my dad in the woods? Had I been possessed by aliens? I do not have the answers and likely never will. But I can tell you with conviction that between church, the movies, and Mom's story of aliens, my love of speculative fiction was cemented for life.

The preacher takes the child by the hand. He leads him up two small steps to a place beside the pulpit and away from the wild congregation still convulsing on the floor.

"Praise Jesus, Mr. Sizemore. Are you ready to accept the Lord into your life?" The preacher's breath reeks of coffee and passion.

"Yes," the child murmurs.

"Praise Jesus! Do you accept that there is only one God and that he gave his only begotten son to save the likes of mankind?"

"Yes."

"Praise Jesus! Do you wish to express your salvation and to be baptized in witness of the Lord and his flock?"

"Yes."

"Let us pray."

The child prays, and imagines a spaceship full of demonically possessed aliens. He vows to write a book about it one day.

I f the Lord set me on the path to aliens, fairies, and gore, then a piece of software pushed me into writing, editing, and publishing.

In the early years of the 21st century, I took a job as the software flunky for the Lexington-Fayette Urban County Government's division of risk management. The work consisted of stereotypical user support. Some examples:

- "Help me, it won't print!"
- "My internet stopped working!"
- "Why did you break my email?"

I also worked at the whim of the director's needs ("Jason, make me a spreadsheet."), and administered and maintained software for my risk management team. The software we used, Risk Master, was—like our director—tedious and annoying. I disliked both, and my co-workers were even less fun.

I hated my job.

On the occasion of my 30th birthday, I found myself working late into the evening. One of our insurance investigators had reported a problem with a monthly report: 49 cents were missing from the prior month's accounts payable. I was elbow deep in the bowels of Risk Master trying to determine whether I had an actual issue or if this was yet another case of user error. My head pulsed with irritation and my eyes strained staring at data for such a long time. From the adjoining office, I could hear the risk management director having a loud conversation with his daughter regarding the best place to have her new Mercedes detailed.

I mumbled angrily to myself like the loser character Milton Waddams from Mike Judge's classic movie *Office Space*. I thought about the huge dent someone had put in the side of my old '87 Chrysler LeBaron while I was inside Walmart the previous weekend.

The director's laughter echoed through the empty offices and hallways. I heard him say good-bye to his spoiled kid.

A few minutes later, the boss walked into my office and leaned against the wall, his arms crossed in a casual stance.

"Are you *still* working on Tom's report?"

I looked up and nodded.

The director checked his watch. He squished up his mousy features in dismay. "Gosh, I need to run. I have a meeting with our realtor in 20 minutes. She's found us a perfect antebellum house in Andover. 4,000 square feet. Five acres of land. Even has a guest house!"

I forced a smile. "That's nice."

The director turned to leave, then paused and looked at me. "You know what I like about you, Sizemore?"

Uh oh, I thought, *where is this heading?* "No, what is it you like about me?"

"You're dependable. Nothing fancy. Nothing memorable. You do your job and you're a professional. Khaki pants. Oxford shirt. Nothing obscene. The last programmer who worked for me was a freak: piercings and tattoos, a—what do you call it?— a tongue stud."

"Thank you. I aim to please."

"Goodnight, young man."

"Goodnight."

Naturally, he had forgotten it was my birthday. I was 30. Still young, but not *so* young anymore.

I mulled over what the director had said. His compliment didn't sit well with me. I didn't want to be 'old reliable' and boring. I wanted to be someone who might make a difference in the world. I wanted to be someone who did interesting work, who could look back on his life and say "This was good." Instead, I sat at a cheap desk, error checking a query due to a 49-cent imbalance for a report that a single, insignificant cog in the city government used once a month. If the insurance investigator was a nobody, what did that make me?

An SQL query I had been running in Risk Master finished, and my computer let out a *ding*.

That audio prompt from Risk Master jarred me awake. My worldview shifted in that moment.

My life would change.

But in what manner?

Having been a heavy reader of science fiction, fantasy, and horror, I followed the genre lit scene closely. I knew that one particularly respected short fiction writer named Christopher Rowe lived in Lexington. I also knew that Christopher and his wife Gwenda Bond ran a small print zine named *Say...* I read every issue of *Say...* they produced. I loved the look of the zine. It was so much prettier than the old dinosaurs[1] you could buy at Barnes & Noble (*Asimov's*, *Analog*, and *F&SF*, specifically). The content was just as good, if not oftentimes better. The stories were edgier and had a more experimental flavor that appealed to my unconventional tastes.

I started to have dangerous visions of new goals and plans. What if somebody produced something like *Say...* and made it available for national distribution? Surely, there had to be an audience for less-traditional speculative fiction than what was printed in the old trade digests. It would be an expensive venture. It would be a risk.

At that time in my life, I needed a place to channel my desire to expand my goals beyond those of 9-to-5 corporate tedium. Running a nationally distributed zine would fulfill me creatively, I decided. It would allow me to feel like I was making a difference in the world in a positive manner by

---

[1] I use this referentially because they've been around for decades, while all other print zines have died off. **(Jason Sizemore)**

providing entertainment to the masses, and as a matter of course, helping authors, editors, and artists make money. I dove headfirst into the business of zine publishing. I read books. I took online courses. I wrote a business plan. I placed a call for stories. Justin Stewart, a graphic designer friend, helped me with the zine layout and provided cover art. I had a zine.

I had an *amazing* zine.

I named it *Apex Science Fiction and Horror Digest,* and it was good.[2]

Unfortunately, my discontent at the day job grew worse. A planned upgrade for Risk Master did not go so well, due to vendor problems and a corrupt database. The director gave me more menial and impossible tasks because of a procedural change within the division of computer science. He ruled over me with a greedy and iron fist.

One sunny spring morning, it all came to a head.

The director had surreptitiously bought himself a cheap, $100 ink jet printer/scanner/fax combo unit on the city's dime. City government policies forbade the purchase of private use equipment even for work purposes. The guy was a stickler for rules, except for when it was an inconvenience.

---

[2] This was 2005, wasn't it? I was an unknown—I'd published a handful of forgettable stories the year before, but this was the year I sort of "broke through" (for a given definition of breaking through), which is something I always associate in part with Apex. I had this weird little short story called "Crucifixation," about Yiddish-speaking robots addicted to religion, in a weird future Jerusalem. There was something about this story that was, well, *me*, in the way the other stories weren't. I just didn't have any idea what to do with it. I saw a listing for *Apex Digest*, which was looking for stories for its first issue, and paid a whole 1c/word(!) and I sent it in on the off chance. There was no one more surprised than I when I got back an e-mail from Jason saying he wanted to publish it—nor did I realize at the time it was the very first story he bought. **(Lavie Tidhar, frequent *Apex SF & Horror Digest* contributor and editor of the *Apex Book of World SF* series)**

Personally, I had no problem with him buying the printer. He had a legitimate need for one. I found the private equipment limitation to be ridiculous, and really, what's $100 to a multi-million dollar government when the money is going to be used for government business only.

On that sunny spring morning, Mr. Director called me into his office.

"Sizemore, can you take a look at my printer?"

"What's wrong with it?"

"The scanner stopped working. Can you see if you can fix it?"

I told him okay and bent down behind his desk where he kept the printer hidden, to investigate. Nothing obvious was wrong. I checked the usual suspects such as the printer driver and the cable connections, and powered it down and back up. Nothing.

"It's broken. There's nothing I can do for it."

"Would you take it to your office and see if you can fix it?"

A few months prior, I had bought a basic computer repair kit with a soldering iron, a few screws and Allen wrenches, and wires. A co-worker's CPU fan had died and I had made a simple fix on my own. This was against city policy where all repairs had to be channeled through the division of computing services, but that would have taken days. I thought I would save everyone a lot of trouble and do it myself.

Being a nice guy never pays.

I took the printer combo unit to my office and messed around with the settings. I was able to make it produce an error code on its display along with two chirps. After a few minutes of research on Google, I discovered that the malfunction was a hardware issue. A chip that could be bought at Radio Shack needed to be replaced.

I reported this to the director.

He took a few bucks from the administrative assistant's petty cash envelope and gave it to me. He instructed me to go to Radio Shack and buy the part.

I thought about the request for a few seconds. Then I declined.

"Why?" he asked.

"Because I don't know how to do hardware repair. It's a cheap printer. You should buy a new one."

"What if I tell you to attempt the repair? If you can't fix it, nothing lost. I'll buy a new one."

I sighed. He was the boss. I was just a computer flunky. "Okay," I said, "but don't get your hopes up."

"You fixed Tom's computer a couple months ago. This should be a piece of cake," he said.

I spent the rest of the morning shopping and taking the printer apart. A website on fixing printer hardware had directions for replacing the malfunctioning chip. I followed the instructions the best I could, but in the end, I had completely ruined the unit. Not only had I not fixed the scanner, but now the fax and print functions no longer worked.

I explained what had happened to the director. His usual calm arrogance had been replaced with a red-faced tantrum.

"*You* broke my printer!"

Shocked, I responded "It was *already* broken! You said you wanted me to *fix* it. You gave me money to *fix* it."

"It worked when you carried it out of my office," he said.

"It was broken. You asked me—no, you *told* me—to work on it," I interjected.

"The printer and fax worked fine and now they don't." He leaned against his desk, arms crossed, smug and overconfident. "Angela, can you come in here for a moment?"

Angela was his admin assistant who worked the front desk. She scurried into the office.

"Yes, sir?"

"Angela, can you verify that the other functions on the printer worked before Jason opened it up?"

The admin assistant nodded. "Yes. I sent a fax on it this morning."

"The fax was fine. You told me to fix the scanner."

"Jason, I see no other recourse than to dock your pay for the cost of the city's equipment you destroyed. Plus the money you spent at Radio Shack."

My mouth gaped open. This was all kinds of ludicrous!

"Nope. No way. You can't do that."

"I'm sorry," the director said, "I can. I know you eastern Kentucky hillbillies[3] don't like being told—"

The anger swelled in me. I tried to hold it back, I really did, but lid was off the pressure cooker. I looked the director square in the eye and gave him the timeless offer to "kiss my ass."

I took an early lunch and came back late. I needed time to cool down, to assess what had happened and what I needed to do to make the predicament better.

On my return to my office, the director stopped me as I exited the elevator and asked me to follow him. "Where are we going?" I asked.

"Downstairs."

I followed, and I had an idea of what I was walking into. We were going to visit an HR mediator to work out the disagreement. The elevator ground to a halt at the HR floor, and we exited. Several nice ladies said hello to us. The whole thing felt unreal. Mr. Director invited me into a nearby office where another friendly, smiling lady sat perched behind a huge, ancient desk. I took a seat and the door closed behind me. The director planted himself in a chair next to me.

The director of human resources introduced herself. I began to have misgivings about the situation, but I continued to be a consummate professional. We shook hands and engaged in some small talk. Eventually, the HR director broached the reason we were meeting in her dark, musty office

"Mr. Sizemore, it has been reported that you have broken government equipment."

---

[3] Hillbilly? Jason's a total city boy! He's got indoor plumbing and I've never once seen him with a coon hound or heard him discussing his need to fabricate parts for a moonshine still! Despite his city-slicker ways, I never once doubted his resourcefulness or determination. **(Lucy A. Snyder, author of the Stoker Award-winning "Magdala Amygdala",** *Dark Faith: Invocations***)**

"Nonsense," I said, interrupting. "You can't break something already broken."

"Furthermore, you've been verbally combative and have been creating a hostile work environment."

I could only laugh. Was this really happening? "Hostile?"

"Yes, your director's administrative assistant reports that you yelled at her."

My temper threatened to go Mount St. Helens inside that tiny room.

"May I have the opportunity to explain my side of the argument?" I asked, plaintively, swallowing the anger.

The HR director nodded and I shared my experiences, right down to the inappropriate use of government funds for the printer.

The HR director looked at my boss. "Is this true? You bought a printer for private use with LFUCG funds?" she asked.

The Director of Risk Management sat straight up in his chair, chin jutted up and outward. "Of course not," he said and sniffed. "My admin assistant can verify that I purchased the printer before the change in policy."

I snorted. "Unbelievable."

That was that. My side of the story was cast aside as falsehoods. The two directors commenced a discussion regarding a six-month probationary period, mandatory anger management counseling, and having my wages garnished an amount equal to the cost it would take to replace the broken printer.

As they discussed punitive actions as though I wasn't sitting *right there*, I considered my life. That exact moment was playing out exactly as it should based on the parameters I had set for myself for the last 30 years. I would sit there meekly, accept whatever punishment deemed appropriate, and continue to being a nobody to all the superiors in my life.

No, that would not do, I thought. I would change the script of my life.

First, though, I had to get these assholes off my back. I stood and gave them official verbal notice of my resignation, effective right goddamn now.

My ex-boss looked dumbstruck. "Now, Jason," he said, hands out in a placating gesture, "don't do anything rash. Nobody wants you to quit. Think about your new baby."

My face burned with contempt and anger. Oh, the things I wanted to say! Instead, I asked, "What about my resignation did you not understand?"

I turned and went to my office to gather my personal items. I offered a brief good-bye to my confused co-workers, and left for good.

I'm not particularly proud or pleased with how my employment with the LFUCG ended. When you have a family, it is never a good idea to quit your job without having a backup plan. Fortunately, we had a safety net of money in the bank, and I landed another, better job as a software developer soon after.

However, the timing of my unemployment could not have been better. The three months between my resignation and the start date of my new position freed me to dedicate many days to producing the next issue of *Apex Digest*. I had the time to make the zine into something that bookstores and newsstands would place on their racks.

Being unemployed also gave me the opportunity to research inexpensive marketing opportunities. During this time, I stumbled upon the notion of fandom conventions. I signed up for the next one occurring in the region: Hypericon in Nashville, TN.

Chapter 2:
The Ham

Having shed the chains of analytical insurance accounting, I took advantage of the free time I now enjoyed. I worked to make issue 2 of *Apex Science Fiction and Horror Digest* twice as awesome as issue 1. Helping me were two extremely talented freelance editors who had joined the team that spring: Deb Taber[4] and Gill Ainsworth. I also landed several supportive and high-paying advertisers that gave me the funds to buy fiction from several Big Name Authors who would draw attention from readers and reviewers and lend credibility to Apex. In a rare stroke of luck, the company that printed my zine messed up the first run of issue 2 so they did a second. I asked them what they would do with the bad copies, which were fine except for faded color on the cover, and they said they would destroy them. I offered to take all copies off their hands for free. I had 1,500 promotional copies of the next issue to give away!

The karma gods looked upon me and said, "We grant him mercy."

I felt momentum building for my zine. The next step would be taking a summer-long promotional road trip, hitting conventions all over the Midwest. The first stop my party wagon would make was Hypericon.

What you're about to read is way out there. Therefore, I feel the

---

[4] My early encounters are a bit of a blur, but they followed the standard scenario that everyone knows: brilliant white light, lost time, moments of bliss alternating with excruciating pain, and afterward, the compulsion to do exactly as my alien overlords required. **(Deb Taber, former senior manager of Apex Publications)**

need to outline certain facts.

1) Hypericon was my first fandom convention. I had attended gamer cons such as Origins and local comic cons numerous times during my years as a semi-professional Magic: The Gathering card player (Yes, I have always been *this* cool.) I thought I knew what to expect at these functions. I thought wrong.

2) The first year I attended Hypericon was also the convention's inaugural year. I'm told Year One of any fandom convention is wacky.

3) They say you'll always remember your first. Well, I had two of the strangest days of my life that weekend. There is no way I will forget what happened, even though I long for the day brain bleach.

4) All Hypericons I've attended since the first one have been professional, fun experiences I would recommend to friends and family alike.

For my first baby steps onto the fandom beachhead, I constructed an unstoppable game plan. I would give away copies of issues 1 and 2 to everyone I met.

Simple goals make for success. Meet people. Be friendly. Shove *Apex Digest* into their hands. But this plan had a major hitch. Like a lot of geeky people, I am an introvert. Handing out copies of *Apex Digest* and talking to attendees required me to engage in conversations. I would have to make cold approaches to strangers—many of them introverts, as well, thereby complicating matters. The thought of all the glad-handing and socializing made me ill and nervous.

But there was no backing out. I'd spent too much money, too much time, and called in too many favors (Hello Justin Stewart, Deb Taber, and Gill Ainsworth![5]) to back out due to

---

[5] Apex always had the approach of "why bother merely attracting people when it's so much better to assimilate them?" Money, fame, basic human comforts—none of those matter when you're a part of the Sizeborg. **(Deb Taber)**

personal anxiety. I might sweat, and I might stammer, but I *would* be there to share with the people the gospel of *Apex Digest*.

The weirdness started a few miles south of the Tennessee/ Kentucky border on my way to Nashville. Thanks to my tiny bladder, I had made a pit stop at a rest area. "Gotta go gotta go gotta go" I chanted as I brushed aside kids and elderly women to make my way to the men's room. Once there, the hallway led to the left and to the right. The right side was closed for maintenance; left it was. A line of men awaited for their turn to do their business.

Finally, my turn. I walked up and faced the open urinal next to an occupied stall. The stall's metal frame was dented and marred with dozens of engraved penises and phone numbers accompanied by messages promising various sexual favors.

I unzipped and was ready to do my business when the man in the stall next to me yelled "Ocupado!" causing me to jump and release an errant stream all over the floor.

Encountering strange behavior in the men's interstate rest areas is not uncommon. I've come to dread these necessary pit stops in the same way that people expect a trip to the DMV to be miserable. My working strategy is to ignore all non-threatening weirdness, do my business, avoid eye contact, and make a hasty retreat.

The acrid scent of cigarette smoke burned my nostrils. A plume of smoke drifted above the confines of the stall. I squished my face in tacit disapproval.

"Hey, pal! The redhead at the urinal!"

I looked around. I was the only red-haired guy lined up facing the wall.

"Hey!" the guy in the stall called out. "You're standing right next to me."

I willed my bladder to work faster. Science has figured out it takes all mammals an average of 21 seconds to pee. Thanks to the weirdo in the stall, I must have been approaching 60 seconds. His attentions had plugged me up like an elderly man dealing with an enlarged prostate.

"Hey, pal!"

I could take no more. "Your pal must have left. I'm the only redhead in the bathroom."

"That's cool, that's cool."

Finished, I zipped up and stepped to the sink.

"Pal, do you mind if I read you some bathroom stall wisdom?"

Busying myself with washing my hands, I mumbled, "Sure thing."

"'Be happy, but not too happy, cuz you'll look like a creeper.'"

True enough, I thought. But I had better places to be than philosophizing with a freak in a public restroom, so I made a hasty exit and continued to Nashville.

Because they're cheap to lease, older hotels and motels are often used to host fan conventions. The organizers of Hypericon hosted the inaugural event in a dump. Seriously, the venue is the worst hotel I've encountered. They held later Hypericons at the same place, but thanks to a few key renovations (removal of foul, moldy carpet, installation of showers that worked, cleaning of rooms) the place became habitable, and not like some skeevy drug din from a 70s grindhouse film.

I checked into the roach motel, got my key, and went to the elevators where I mashed the call button. Seconds later, the doors slid open to the surprise of two women inside.

"Are we on the ground floor? We're on the ground floor. The elevator should have taken us to the top," complained a dark-skinned, dark-eyed brunette.

"Don't complain. I expected this thing to open into a Lovecraftian den." The second woman spoke with an educated, self-assured manner. She had fiery hair and a slightly bemused expression.

"Come in, we promise it's not safe."

I pushed my suitcase and myself into the elevator.

"Fifth floor," I croaked.

"Aww, this one's nervous."

The redhead grinned. "No sudden movements or we'll spook him."

True. My lizard brain screamed "Flee!" but my practical side said "Talk." I would be social. I would not be an introvert. I would not be frightened of nice people. I would promote Apex.

I summoned the courage to speak. "It's my first con," I said.

"A con virgin!" declared the brunette.

They both laughed.

"I'm Jason Sizemore. Hi." I proffered my sweaty hand.

The brunette smiled. I noticed she had glitter on her face. Lots and lots of glitter. It suited her. "My name is Alethea. Princess Alethea Kontis." She had the friendliest smile I'd ever seen. My social confidence meter spiked upward.

The redhead took my hand and held it. "I'm Sherrilyn Kenyon." I recognized her name—she wrote popular paranormal romance novels available at my local Kroger. Ten minutes in and I had met a famous author.

I felt a bit star struck. After an uncomfortable moment, I felt compelled to say something... anything.

"I, uh, publish a zine." I fumbled around in the depths of my backpack and withdrew two copies of *Apex Digest*.

Alethea gasped. "No. Way. Is that *Apex Digest*?"

Sherrilyn raised an eyebrow and looked questioningly at Alethea.

"I bought both issues from your website. I haven't read them yet, but they're gorgeous!"

I blushed worse than a schoolboy caught peeking up his 5th grade teacher's skirt.

Sherrilyn flipped through issue 2. "This is nice. Did you do all this on your own?"

"I did. Well, I mean I had help, but I did most of the pro-duction work."

The elevator chimed. The doors ground open.

"It's a miracle—the top floor." The ladies exited.

Sherrilyn looked back at me and winked. "Perhaps I'll have to come up with something for your zine."

"Yes, please," I called out as the doors shut.

The elevator had skipped my floor. I pressed 5 again and did a private victory dance

That Friday night and the following Saturday afternoon I attended several panel discussions. Authors such as Brian Keene, Tom Piccirilli, Scott Nicholson, Sherrilyn Kenyon, Tim Waggoner, and Bryan Smith were dropping the gospel like a group of publishing evangelicals.[6]

Throughout the day, I gave *Apex Digest* to dozens of attendees. Despite congenital shyness, I spoke with people and made valiant attempts at conversation. People were impressed with my publication. That afternoon, I encoun-tered Alethea in the con suite and we had a wonderful conversation about our occupations. I told her I was an out-of-work software developer. She disclosed that she worked for Ingram Book Distribution and that she knew someone on the magazine side of the business whom I could speak with regarding national distribution for *Apex Digest*.

That evening, after dinner, I attended an entertaining bur-lesque show as part of the convention festivities. After the show ended and the crowd departed, I overheard several dis-cussions concerning a party floor. *Wow*, I thought, *a whole level*

---

[6] I can't remember when I first met Jason, but my earliest memories of him are seeing him speak on panels at conventions. Unlike other panelists who might show up drunk, Jason, ever the multitasker, would bring booze with him—usually one of those frou-frou drinks that are colored red, has big chunks of fruit it in, and has a tiny paper umbrella sticking out of the top. (**Tim Waggon-er, author of** *Like Death*)

of a hotel committed to fraternizing and fun! Dumpy hotels are the best! I asked a tiny elderly lady standing nearby which level the parties were going down.

"Eighth floor."

"Thanks," I said, turning to leave.

Something grabbed my elbow. Hard. I twisted around. The elderly lady had me in a vice grip and glared at me fiercely.

"Don't eat the ham."

"What ham?" I demanded.

She released me and disappeared into the crowd. I rubbed my arm, grimacing. I loved ham. What was her problem?

I made my way to the eighth floor where I found a bustle of activity. The hallway was filled with open rooms and people engaging in loud conversations. Most had free alcohol available, so I grabbed a cup of random beer and wandered about. I offered a copy of *Apex Digest* to anyone who looked at me. A guy handing out free reading materials makes many friends among a crowd of book geeks. Go figure.

I ventured further down the hallway where I came upon another opened door. Inside, a group of writers huddled in the back of the room. It appeared as though one author, Brian Keene, was holding court. He pontificated on some arcane publishing matter. I stepped inside without provocation.

At first, nobody noticed the shy redhead in the corner. I listened as Mr. Keene railed against an unnamed editor who owed him (and others) money. Brian abruptly ended the discussion, turned to me and asked "Who the fuck are you?"

"J-J-J-ason Sizemore."

"This is a private party. I'm going to ask you to leave."

I shifted my backpack and turned to go.

"It's okay, Brian, he's cool."

I looked around for the source of the voice. Sitting among the group pressed tightly around Brian was that glitterbomb of cuteness—Princess Alethea Kontis.

"That's the *Apex Digest* guy I was telling you about."

My mouth felt dry and filled with cotton. I recognized many in Brian's group: Tom Piccirilli, Bryan Smith, Scott Nicholson, James Moore, and Deborah Leblanc. Tom Piccirilli, in particular, looked imposing. In reality, Tom is a great guy—kind and generous—but at the time I did not possess this important knowledge.

Brian's face lit up. "No shit? This is *Apex Digest*?"

"Yes, sir," I said.

The crowd laughed at that. "*Sir?*" Brian chuckled at the word. "Where did you find this one, Lee? He talks funny. Sort of like Bryan."

Bryan Smith, a reserved and withdrawn writer from Tennessee, nodded.

"He sort of appeared on the elevator."

"Have some Bald Knob Bourbon," Brian offered, "and tell us about *Apex Digest*."

I took a spot on the bed, handed out copies of *Apex Digest* and shared my hopes and dreams as they flipped through the issues. For hours, we talked the vagaries of running a small zine, and I received a wheelbarrow-full of industry knowledge from some of the smartest writers in the business.

Hours later, blissful and exhausted, I made to leave. On the way out, Tom Piccirilli took me aside.

"Look, I want to help you out. I might have a story I can send you, you pay me what you can, just don't tell anyone. As far as the world knows, I squeezed you for my usual rate. Right?"

"Right—"

"The zine's not perfect. It's a bit rough around the edges, if you know what I mean. But I can tell you're trying to do this the right way. Writers appreciate that. So don't fuck this up."

I gulped. "No, sir, I won't."

Tom shook his head. "You and your fucking 'sirs'."

A week after Hypericon I received a fantastic dystopian science fiction piece from Tom.

I had a big head. My confidence reached stratospheric levels after my night with Keene's group. I walked around reliving the compliments and praise in my head.

An elderly couple interrupted my stupor to ask if I had any copies of *Apex Digest* on me.

"Sure thing let me…."

They were each clad head to toe in black leather. The woman held a long black crop in one hand and a silver chain in the other that led to a studded collar clipped tightly around the man's neck. I took a step back, trying to process the scene. I'd never witnessed an old man being led around like a slave.

"Um, here you go," I said.

The lady smiled. "Oh, they're soooo nice," she cooed.

"Enjoy," I croaked.

"I *take* my enjoyment." She placed the end of the crop on my forehead. "And my pleasure."

"Yes, ma'am."

Until that moment, I hadn't considered that BDSM would be part of a fan literary convention. I'm still not sure.

I backed up and bumped into a short, silver-haired woman. She might have been somebody's dear grandmother—the type to give you a quarter and a handful of hard candy whenever you visited.

Still rattled, I said, "Excuse me."

She grabbed my arm. "Oh my, you look overwhelmed."

"It's been a crazy day."

The sweet old lady smiled. "That's why we have a room dedicated to the art of relaxation. Would you like to come inside? We have food and drinks."

I had driven to Nashville to meet people, befriend genre fans. Turning away an invitation would be contrary to my goals, so I said, dumbly, "Okay, sure."

"Good. Come inside."

I walked into a two room suite. In one half of the suite was the usual accoutrements: dressers, desk and chair, television, a couch. On the desk was a small spread of drinks and cheeses. In the middle of the room on a small fold-out card table rested the largest honey-baked ham I'd ever seen. Pieces of food detritus lay scattered all around its platter and littered the floor.

Odd noises, like the rhythmic slapping of meat on meat, played from the other half of the suite. Seventies R&B played on a stereo. I peered inside. Five people on a king-sized bed, all naked, were engaged in group coitus. Two men. Three women.

For the first time in my life, I bore witness to an orgy.

A nude gentlemen who I did not recognize, paused mid-thrust and waved at me. "Hey, it's *Apex Digest*! Come join us!" His voice sounded familiar. A huge creepy smile adorned his face.

If I joined that crowd, I would have been the youngest by twenty years, at least. I stepped back, and looked at the lady who had invited me inside. "Is this some type of joke?"

She put on a hurt face. "Of course not. As you can see, they need a third male."

By now, I had knocked into the room's door and was groping around for the handle.

"Don't you want to eat something, first? The ham is delicious."

No. I would not have any ham. The juxtaposition of human thighs and honey-baked ham made me blanch.

I wrenched the door opened and rushed out of there.

Apex Digest thrived due to the connections I made at Hypericon. Alethea Kontis hooked me up with Ingram Periodicals and we landed distribution with the next issue. Many authors I met that weekend would appear in future issue.

That weekend, I also learned that the 'buddy' system applies to fandom conventions. You need someone by your side to bear witness to the wackiness that happens. You need someone by your side to tell you when going into a stranger's room is a bad idea.

Chapter 3:
A Forgotten Night

Those who know me well observe that I have three superpowers. That's three more than most get and two more than I want.

Superpower 1: The ability to find incredibly intelligent, motivated, and energetic young people to assist me with Apex Publications. Without these hard-working and kind souls, there would be no ten years of Apex. I would be just another mediocre code monkey sheltered away in a dark, windowless office, cursing at black and green mainframe screens. As the years wore on, my pale features would go from "Wow, he's pale even for a redhead!" to "Hey, who let Gollum out of his cage?"

Whatever it is that inspires such wonderful people to work with Apex so diligently, I do not know. I only know that I am thankful beyond measure.

Between me and you, I would have been happy with one superpower. Asking for anything more is being presumptuous and greedy. Receiving more than one is playing loaded dice with the karma gods. I'm certain these gods of luck and fortune have looked down upon me and realized "Hey, that red bastard is due three superpowers. This must not stand!" and imprinted their wrath in fair measure on my poor soul. It's the only way I can explain the last two superpowers.

Superpower 2: A preternatural knack for flipping nickels. I've no idea why I can do this. It serves no purpose. As a party trick, it barely amuses even the drunkest of fools. Most people who have watched me in action do not believe in my knack and accuse me of tomfoolery. During my college years, I landed some amazing shots. Across-the-room flips that miraculously plunked firmly in small Solo cups. Launching nickels into the pockets of receivers twenty feet away.

I do have to keep my nickel-flipping skills polished. I can't go three months without flipping, walk into a bar, and ping a nickel off some tattooed biker's head across the way. It takes a bit of practice—perhaps a couple hours a week. Because I'm too lazy to put in the time to stay sharp, I have lost the skill.

Superpower 3: The second power is harmless and passive. A waste of a superpower, certainly, but nothing that's upsetting. This third one has plagued me relentlessly and, unfortunately for me, it grows stronger as the years roll by. The equation plays out like this: place Jason Sizemore in location X and individual Y with the highest annoyance potential will be drawn to me. Like two opposite ends of a magnet. Like summertime mosquitos to a sweaty, shirtless child. Like office drones to free pizza. Like cheapskates to Black Friday sales.

All three of my considerable powers exerted themselves at Conglomeration, the second fandom convention I attended. After the honey-baked ham episode, I learned the value of the buddy system. I needed a person who could provide a buffer between the convention weirdness and the innocent Appalachian upbringing that made me susceptible to dangerour situations.

That person was Justin Stewart.

Justin Stewart is a talented graphic designer and artist. The unique visual style of Apex Publications is his creation. Justin crafted and designed the covers for the first two issues of *Apex Science Fiction and Horror Digest* to help out a cash strapped young publisher buddy (see Superpower #1).

The other thing that makes Justin useful? The guy is unflappable.

No matter how strange or terrifying a situation becomes, he cannot be rattled. I'd discovered this in the early days of Apex, when Justin accompanied me to Chattacon.

Apex had a table in the dealer's hall and across from us, an indie film director named Glen Weiss had space to promote his short film *Thong Girl*. The five-minute trailer for Thong Girl played on a 13" color television on permanent loop. As you might surmise, what the movie lacked in talent, it contained in laughs. The highlight of the trailer indisputably was a scene where the heroic Thong Girl (dressed in a red cape, a red bikini top, and, yes, a red thong) uses her 'super thong' to stop a steaming locomotive from running down a fey man tied to the rails. In the scene, the young superhero hikes up her cape, bends down, and blasts a laser beam from the thong, sending hundreds of tons of steel to oblivion and saving the day.

Justin and I watched this scene play out more than 100 times over the weekend.

The actress who played Thong Girl in the film, Leah Adcock, worked the director's table much of the weekend. She wore the Thong Girl costume and an expression of a lady who wanted to be doing anything else with her life other than playing Thong Girl. To that end, I couldn't blame her.

As the dealer's room wound down Sunday afternoon , I decided to talk with her about the movie and ask how she got involved in its production. I wanted to know how a person gets chosen to be a thong-wearing superwoman.

I sauntered over and started a conversation. Justin stayed seated at our table.

"So, uh, hello."

Leah looked up at me. She started to smile, then stopped. "Hello," she said.

"I'm Jason Sizemore. With Apex Publications. We have the table directly across from yours." I pointed across the aisle, as though she had somehow missed the two goofballs sitting in front of her for the past three days.

"Sure. You're friends with the guy wearing the unicorn shirt. It's cool."

(Okay, a quick aside—at Chattacon, Justin wore a pink T-shirt that bore a picture of two unicorns procreating underneath a glorious rainbow. To this day people ask me about my friend with the unicorn shirt.)

"Right," I said. "That's my artist friend, Justin Stewart."

I saw that she had promotional shots of herself as Thong Girl available at her table in front of her. I took one and asked her to sign it.

"That'll be five dollars."

I frowned. The picture wasn't glossy. It was matte and quite fuzzy. Obviously a DIY production. I've no problem with DIY, but I felt five dollars was rather steep.

"Five dollars?"

"For five dollars, you'll get the picture signed, and I'll show you the Super Thong." She kept it discreetly hidden by her long red cape.

Justin appeared beside me like a magical ninja. He snapped a crisp, new five dollar bill between his two thumbs and forefingers. "I'll take that offer."

Leah took the money, signed a photo, and motioned for Justin to follow her behind a red cloth screen. Alone. A moment passed and they reappeared, Justin smiling like someone had just handed him a bottle of his favorite beer.

Justin slapped me on the shoulder. "When life hands you a thong, well... you know...."

No, I did not know. I still do not know.

"Did you really see the thong?" I asked.

He said gentleman didn't share such matters, and that was that. Like I said: unflappable. A quality that served me well later at Conglomeration.

I bought an autographed photo from Ms. Adcock for five bucks anyway.

Leah Adcock as Thong Girl

On our arrival at the Conglomeration venue hotel, Justin hopped out of the car saying he needed to go squirt (Justin speak for going to the men's room). I decided to take our two boxes of *Apex Digest* to our table and register. Just as I stepped inside the hotel lobby, an ear-piercing alarm erupted. Hotel staff politely informed everybody that we needed to step outside and wait for the fire trucks to arrive.

A crowd of several hundred people milled around the parking lot under a hot summer sun. Close by, a drunk guy made loud demonstrative declarations of unhappiness. At some point he spotted me.

I stood as far from the entrance and the drunken guy as I could manage without looking suspicious. The effort was for naught, as I was soon accosted by the stink of cheap whiskey and the attentions of a man bearing angry indignation. The guy didn't wear a shirt. A messy mullet adorned his shoulders.

"Can you believe this bullshit?"

The guy must have been circling the drain of consciousness. He slurred. He stumbled. He carried a brown paper bag that held his whisky.

"You know what?" he asked, rhetorically. "I was naked, ready to take a shower, when the alarm went off. Scared the piss out of me. I nearly broke my neck reaching for my piece."

"That's unfortunate," I mumbled.

He elbowed me roughly in the arm then grabbed his crotch. "And buddy ,I ain't talking about this piece."

"Right."

I looked for an escape. Unfortunately, being new to the fandom scene, I didn't know a single person outside with me.

"Worst part is, I'm not even supposed to be here. I was in lockup just...." He looked at a cheap gold watch on his wrist. "... just three hours ago."

"Lockup?"

"Yeah, my PO told me to come by the hotel. He'd booked me a room."

"That was nice of him."

"I'm in my room, watching Fox News, when a woman knocked on the door. Now she ain't the prettiest thing I've seen, but I let her in. You know what? My uncle Leroy hired me an escort. Now ain't that the craziest shit you ever heard?"

Eyebrow raised, I said, "That is."

The guy took a drink from the bottle, slapped me on the back, and started to laugh. "I'm bullshitting you, son. Don't be so goddamn gullible."

Justin appeared right then. "Drained the lizard. Ready to carry shit to our table, chief?"

"I already carried it in," I said.

He looked from me to the drunk, then back to me. "You didn't get my box."

Now I understand his meaning. I nodded and followed as Justin walked away. He had opened the trap door and set me free.

The convention had seen fit to place the Apex table outside the actual exhibit hall. While we didn't have to watch the cinematic masterwork that was the *Thong Girl* trailer, this time, we were located next to a loquacious older gentleman who had books of every kind on his table: comic books, graphic novels, DIY chapbooks, novels, magazines, etc. Almost all of them had animated-style covers of anthropomorphized animals in various stages of undress and sexual activities.

On the Apex table were the first two issues of *Apex Digest*. I felt as bare and exposed as the little squirrels and rabbits adorning the books next to me.

Being the naïve and arrogant guy I am, I thought to myself "Who buys this shit?" I'd seen the *CSI* episode about furries. But Conglomeration was in Louisville, and Louisville is in Kentucky, and there sure as shit weren't any fans of sexy anthropomorphic animals in Kentucky that I knew about.

I was wrong. So very wrong.

Justin and I sold eight copies of the zine that weekend. Our neighbor sold dozens upon dozens of naughty cartoon stories. In particular, a graphic novel about a well-endowed horny squirrel caught the eye of many customers. His wad of cash (that he kept waving at us) grew fatter as time passed.

In the end, I bought one of his books and had him sign it. It rests in a place of honor in my office, next to my signed photo of Thong Girl.

At this Conglomeration I met the man I call Hickory Adams. I'm terrible with names, and I simply cannot remember Hickory's real name. I do recall it being the name of a tree, but which tree that was… alas, I do not know. And there's no way I'm asking the guy.

I was at the Apex table doing my best to ignore a perverted hippie commune my neighbor was sharing with a customer when a short, elderly guy gripping a set of thick spiral bound notebooks approached and reached his hand out to me. I took it and offered a warm greeting.

"Nice to meet you, Mr. Sizemore," he said.

Thanks to my early mid-life crisis, I hated being called Mr. Sizemore. I insisted he call me Jason.

"I'm Hickory Adams. I want to pitch you a collection of my short fiction."

"I'm sorry, Hickory—"

"Young man, the students in my class call me Mr. Adams and I must insist you do the same."

His tone caught me off guard. "Oh, uh, sorry, Mr. Adams. I don't publish books. Apex only publishes a magazine." I held out issue 1 of *Apex Digest* helpfully.

"Is that right?"

"Yep."

He placed the notebooks on my table and opened the top one. "All my stories are all horror themed. In the first one—"

"Mr. Adams," I interrupted, "we don't publish books."

"—we meet a group of socially conscious kids who organized an attack against this country's fine servicemen and women. The other stories deal with each kid separately and how our honorable military snuff out these traitors to our country."

I looked at him. I didn't know what to say—that it sounded like North Korean propaganda?

"Would you consider serializing them in the magazine?"[7]

"Not a chance," I said.

---

[7] Being persistent as a writer is a valuable personal trait, but… **(Jason Sizemore)**

That first Conglomeration will always hold a tender spot in my heart because of the many writers, artists, and industry peers I met that would play important parts in Apex and my life. Included among this lot was Judi Davidson, who would go on to do the cover art for the third book I published (*Temple: Incarnations* by Steve Savile). This was where I met Paul and Michael Bielaczyc, brothers who ran an art studio together and have done numerous covers for our books and the zine. In the early days of Apex, we had a spokesmodel named Amanda Dailey. Amanda has become a good friend of mine and we stay in touch even though she's moved on to grander occupations. I also made the acquaintance of Melissa Gay, another mega-talented artist who created the popular covers to Lavie Tidhar's *HebrewPunk* and Sara Harvey's trio of novellas.

Conglomeration was also where I learned the art of moderation when it comes to enjoying libations at a public event. Because of my sheltered upbringing and conservative college lifestyle, this was not a life skill I had picked up during my formative early years.

You have to be careful at conventions. There are these things called room parties. Perhaps they would be better named Free Alcohol Refreshment Stations. You walk into a hotel room where a party is hosted. Sometimes you go to a bar (usually the hotel room's desk or credenza) and pick up a free beer or a cup of inexpensive booze. Other times, you're handed a cup of unknown contents and told to enjoy. That particular evening, I remember a bearded giant of a man who offered me something called The Blue Stuff from a large orange cooler he toted across his chest. I liked how the blue stuff tasted... sort of a tasty mix of blue Kool-Aid and weak cough syrup. I asked for seconds. Justin strongly urged me off a second serving.

I ignored Justin the Wise. He shook his head in disappointment.

🛸

Frankly, I have no memory of that Saturday night after about 10 p.m.

I woke up the next day thanking the heavens that I was safely in my room, fully dressed, face down on my bed and not face down and dead in a water-filled ditch somewhere with my pants around my ankles.

Lessons learned: Steer clear of the blue stuff. Exercise the liver more. Listen to Justin Stewart's suggestions.

♥

Once I had gathered my senses, I noticed that Justin was not in the room. It was 8 a.m., so I doubted he had risen early that morning to find breakfast. He had not left a note, and none of his belongings appeared to have been touched since the previous day. I decided to shower and then venture out to look for my buddy.

Justin wasn't in the con suite (for the uninitiated, this is a suite of free snacks and beverages provided by convention officials for attendees). He wasn't in the convention halls. By this point I'm a bit worried. What would I tell his wife? What would I tell his dog? "Sorry, a hirsute mountain of a man got me drunk and stole off with him."

I went back to the hotel room, and there he was. Clean, fresh, and ready to go. Like always.

"Dude. I thought you were in jail or something. Where did you go?" I asked.

Justin smiled. "Around midnight, your drunken ass insisted on coming back to the room to go to bed. We laid you down and left."

"We? Did we make friends?"

"Nah. Just some guys. After we put you to bed, we went to a karaoke bar. I got to sing 'Bad Touch' by The Bloodhound Gang. You've really not lived until you hear a group of Latinos sing 'Head Like a Hole.'"

Admittedly, fandom is not the most diverse of cultures.

Conglomeration that year was no exception to this rule. I remembered seeing few minorities in attendance, let alone a group of Latinos.

"You're kidding with me. Your eyes aren't even bloodshot."

"No way, man. It all went down like I said."

"Maybe you can introduce me to your friends before we leave? I'll believe you then."

"Can't do that, bro-man. They left this morning. Right before I came back to the room. We gotta roll, sucka, the dealer's room opens in ten minutes."

Much of that weekend no longer exists in my memory, if it ever did. I survived because of the unflappable Justin Stewart. The guy is a prime example of my first superpower in action. He's also seen the third superpower in action and has helped me out of a number of difficult situations. Perhaps, as a way of thanking him, one day I will save his life with a well-placed nickel flip.

A Forgotten Night
Eyewitness Rebuttal

Justin Stewart

First, thanks to young Mr. Sizemore for the kind words regarding me and my constitution. It's much appreciated, sir.

Second, it was a blue shirt that featured two unicorns going to plow town. Not a pink one. But I understand facts can get hazy when recalling the past.

Third, when it comes to the details of that first Conglomeration Jason and I shared, well, let's just say he and I had different, yet similar experiences. Yes, Jason did imbibe in too much of The Blue Stuff. Jason did not have the knowledge of "If it ain't yours, you'll kiss the floor" wisdom of booze consumption. I was able to wrangle him into our hotel room before shenanigans were had and put him in bed shortly thereafter. I was aided in this by artist Judi Davidson. So Jason recalls me saying "we" in reference to "guys you'll meet soon," when I meant "we" as in Judi Davidson and myself. I may not have made that clear at the time.

Anyway, I went out to an open area where most of the partying had been taking place. There I saw a guy I could not remember seeing before when Jason and I were getting Blue'd or at the con earlier.

I said, "Hey. What's up? I'm Justin."

He said, "I'm Jorge."

I said, "Cool man. You get any of that Blue Stuff?"

He smirked and chuckled something to the effect of, "Nah, I partied earlier in my room."

"Oh, right on," I kicked back.

"Still have some, if you want to check out what no one's got out here," he replied.

Now after that statement, Jorge made a hand gesture to let me know that everything was "Okay." Although in retrospect, his representation of the letter O was a bit more pointed than I'm accustomed to seeing.

Anyway, I said, "Let's check it out."

Justin Stewart and his unicorns.

No one really wants to know the details of the rest of this story. However, I will say Jorge was a right proper host. He offered me some Mexican beer I'd never seen before, tequila, and…we'll say "cookies." He, his friend Marcos, and I just kicked it and hung out with our beer, tequila, and cookies. Afterwards, we went to a karaoke bar and pretty much shut that place down with our moves and voices. We came back to the hotel where I bade them a 'good night/morning' and they did the same. I walked to the hotel room where I found Jason had NOT moved at all, at any point, while I was gone. He had Blue'd himself thoroughly. His button-up shirt front pocket had dribbled about 30 nickels onto the bedspread. I did take a moment to allow myself to say, "I told you so," while finger-gun pointing at his black Asics still on his feet.

The bond that happened then is one of the tent poles of our relationship, and I thank Jason for sharing that with me—no matter how porous his recall of that convention has become.

Or, for that matter, however much I remember of it. The details of what actually happened can be debated, but the thing that happened without a doubt is I got to have an experience because of Jason and because of Apex that I had never had before. It set me on a path I'm still on today, and will be on until Thong Girl can't stop the runaway train that left the station that weekend.

When people learn you're the editor of a short fiction magazine, they press you for all the lurid slush pile stories. They understand that the world overflows with twisted, confused individuals and that, as an editor, you have chosen to make your living with the creative output from that crowd. Due to ghastly curiosity, they have questions.

What's the craziest story you've ever received?
Oh, I'll get to that later.

Have you ever read anything that made you want to call the police?
No. But other things related to editing have. I'll get to that later, too.

Has anybody famous ever submitted a story?
Stephen King, if you're reading this, I'm still waiting for your story.

Any experienced editor who works with a slush pile will have a litany of odd encounters to share. It's part of the burden of working with the public-at-large. The privilege of working with the 'outside the bell curve' types is a necessary part of the job.

The boring truth is that most slush stories are simply unremarkable. You read them, you reject them, you move on to the next one. But once in a while, strange and unfortunate stories find their way to the submission stacks like fruit gnats magically appearing around your kitchen table.

Lesson one as editor: Don't place your home address in the magazine's masthead. I did just this in the first two issues of *Apex Digest*. I had yet to learn the hard lesson that some people accept rejection in less-than-professional ways.[8]

I received my first threat of violence (this implies more than one because, of course, there *has been* more than one) while reading submissions for the third issue of *Apex Digest*. Years of managing a small business has taught me that a smart business tactic is to always be a professional, so my rejections are concise, short, and polite. Should the mood hit, I'll include personal feedback, particularly to authors I know personally and won't take my suggestions as an insult. However, a majority of the time I'll send a form rejection. Not because I don't like to help people with their writing, but more as a matter of personal time restrictions. Form letters are an evil necessity in the publishing business.

A form rejection ignited one man's irrational anger in a memorable and frightening way. Six minutes after I emailed the rejection notice, the author wrote a heated response.

Before I go any further, let me give writers these words of advice: *never, ever respond to a rejection*. You're not going to change anybody's mind. Move on and try again with a different story.

Also before I go any further, let me give editors these words of advice: *never, ever respond to a rejection response*. The writer at the other end of the letter is likely in an emotional and irrational state. Move on, you have hundreds of stories waiting for you in the slush pile.

At that point of my editing career, I had never received an argumentative, impassioned response to a rejection. Perhaps a few "Thank you for your consideration" and "Maybe next time" notes here and there, sure—harmless stuff that wasted my time. But this author had a beef with me over a most unusual thing.

I've always worked hard to make sure Apex has a reasonable

---

[8] By the time I came along, Jason *had* figured everything out. Except how to pronounce "Glossolalia." The hillbilly still has no idea what he's doing there. **(Janet Harriett, senior editor of Apex Publications)**

response time. Back in those halcyon times, my goal was to answer all submissions within seven days. I had rejected this upset gentleman's story in two days. Two days! The author's polemic made it clear he felt that two days was not sufficient time to read, assess, and reject his story. He then went on to say mean things about *Apex Digest* and said he wiped his ass with the pages of my zine.

I wondered then and I wonder now: who gets upset over a two-day response time? I've had publications hold on to my work for two years before they reject it. Compared to that, two days seems like a minor miracle. And if you hate a magazine enough to wipe off your derriere with it, why submit your work to us? Trust me there are more derriere friendly options available in the personal hygiene aisle.

Being naïve and a bit brash, I wrote him back, providing a moderately polite, yet stern explanation of why his story didn't work for me, of how great it should feel to receive a response in two days, and why he might wish to refrain from making accusations and insults.

The guy pounced back in mere minutes. I'm going to paraphrase his letter:

Dear Mr. Sizemore,

The arrogant tone you take with me indicates a dismissive nature. I don't let anybody talk to me that way. Not my wife. Not my own daddy. And especially I won't let it happen with you.

I should remind you that I know where you live. It's in every issue of your precious magazine I've seen. In fact, I've been past your house on several occasions. If you had taken the time to read my submission, you would have seen that I live in Lexington, too. Do me a favor. The next time your kids are outside playing in the yard, you remember that I might be watching.

Sincerely,
XXXXX XXXXXX

FOR EXPOSURE

Personal threats have never bothered me. As a certified Kentucky redneck, I've been in plenty of altercations. But to have a crazy guy insinuating harm to my family scared me. And the reason for the threats? I had rejected his story too quickly. I considered giving the Lexington police our correspondence just in case, but in the end I didn't. Perhaps I should have.

I blocked the guy on all my personal and business accounts and hoped he would go away. Fortunately, that appears to be the case, as I never heard from him again, unless he submits work under a pseudonym.

Between the release of issues 1 and 2, I realized I needed help with the slush. In a case of wildly fantastic luck, I made friends with a British writer and editor named Gill Ainsworth. She's a few years older than me, but we were like two peas in a pod. Our personalities and corresponding sense of humor matches well. We just click. I don't recall how I discovered that she was a talented copy and line editor... perhaps it was in a cover letter to one of her submissions. In any case, I asked her to join the team, to be a part of the Apex Global Empire. She accepted.[9]

As Gill and I read for issue 3 over the Christmas holiday, she shared a submission that still makes my stomach turn when I think about it.

Some groundwork needs to be laid so that you'll compre-

---

[9] Way back in the Year of 'When I Was Lots, Lots Younger!' that happened to coincide with the Year of 'Apex Global Domination Starts Here!' I wrote an e-mail along the lines of:

Dear Mr Sizemore, Would you please consider [my latest short] for publication...?

The reply came quickly: Thank you for your submission, but I'm afraid it isn't quite right for *Apex Digest* [or something along those lines but definitely phrased more politely]. And then the e-mail continued with something akin to: However, would you consider [see, so polite!] a job as a slush reader [for that read Brit-Editor-to-Be]?

To which I replied: Well, I'm English and I spell words differently from you... And let's not mention punctuation!

'You got the job!' he replied by return. **(Gill Ainsworth, the original Apex minion)**

hend an appropriate level of grotesquery on display. There's a filmmaker named Fred Vogel who in 2001 directed a disgusting pseudo-snuff film titled *August Underground* (and its two sequels). The IMDB synopsis of *August Underground* states: "Two serial killers go on a murdering rampage as one films the outcome from behind a cheap video camera." The movie's tagline is "The sickest film ever made." Having watched it, I can say it *is* the sickest film I've ever watched. Other than a few botched special effects, the whole thing feels real enough to make you want a hot shower.

The story that Gill had sent me as a Christmas 'gift' would make Fred Vogel proud.

To preserve the innocence of any untainted souls reading this, I'm going to make my description as straightforward and gore-free as possible. Or you can play it safe and skip to the next section.

The story: A guy is driving home late one night from a rock gig. Along the way, something falls out of the sky and lands in front of his massive Cadillac. A huge impact crater is created in the road. The man, who is drunk and stoned, gets out of his car and discovers a beast that resembles a demon: horns, red skin, and cloven hooves. The demon's body is busted up from the fall and it appears to be dead, but the rocker plays it safe, takes out his guitar from the backseat and gives the demon a bloody beating that would feel at home in Mel Gibson's *Passion of the Christ*. Satisfied, the guy throws the body of the demon into his trunk and continues his drive home. Along the way, perhaps drawn by the demon's body stink or blood, animals of all varieties jump in front of the Cadillac. The rocker mows them down, relishing the crunch and 'thunk thunk' of God's creations under his wheels. Rabbits. Cats. Deer. Multiple foxes. Dogs. Frogs. He finally reaches home and drives his gore covered vehicle into a garage attached to the house. The unfortunate reader discovers that the rocker lives with his grandmother when she dodders through the doorway and he demands she help him with the 'meat'. Together, they hoist the demon from the trunk and cast him to the floor.

Something unholy happens involving the demon, the rocker, and grandma.

Thinking about this abomination makes me want to return to Preacher Hayes' church in Big Creek and plead to the Good Lord to have mercy on mankind.

Readers and writers often query me regarding the pathway from submission to publication. The peek behind the curtain is much less glamorous than many think.

Cover art by Loika

It all starts with the writers. They submit work to the magazine. Lots and lots of writers do this. When I tell someone that *Apex Magazine* (the current, digital-only, incarnation of *Apex Science Fiction and Horror Digest*) has 21 submissions editors, a managing editor, and an editor-in-chief, they stare at me in disbelief. They want to know why the heck we have so many people on the team. As of April, 2015, our zine receives on average 800-1,000 submissions a month. Distribute that evenly to 21 slush readers and each editor has to plow through approximately 50 stories. Lesley Conner, our managing editor, reads the stories that are passed up to the next level. These she filters for quality control and sends to me. There are a small number of writers that are allowed to submit directly to me. On average, I read and consider 25 high-quality shorts a month.

Of those 25 stories, I'll usually reject all but five. The last five I'll hold for two additional weeks. I'll read them again. I'll compare them to stories we've published in the recent past and stories we have scheduled to be published in the future. Sadly, this process will occasionally exclude fantastic stories. For example, I recently had to turn away a fantastic circus-themed fantasy piece because we have one in our inventory and we published another in the previous issue. You know how it goes, too many clowns and readers will complain. Weighing all these factors, I'll decide on the best of the *best-fitting* two or three stories and make an offer of publication to the authors.

I say 'offer of publication' because there have been times where a story will be accepted and the author informs us that the story has already been sold elsewhere. Sometimes a withdrawal notice is missed. Sometimes an author makes a mistake and doesn't realize he or she has simultaneously subbed to two or more publications. Sometimes an author simply doesn't care about the guidelines.

When I have any major development edit requests, I make them prior to my offer to publish. Generally, it goes something like "So, hey, if you can clean up this one big plot hole to our satisfaction, then we'll buy your story." However, this does not happen often. Most of the time, the best three stories out of 1,000 submissions will be near-ready for publication upon submission.

If the author accepts our offer of publication, things move quickly from there. The managing editor will send the author a contract for publication. Once signed, authors are encouraged to announce his or her sale to *Apex Magazine*. The more they brag, the happier I am.

The stories are copy edited (red-line edits). These edits are sent to the authors for review and approval. As an inexperienced editor, I once made the mistake of copy editing a story and publishing it without running the changes past the author. That was a memorable, unprofessional, rookie mistake I won't make again. The internet shaming I received still hurts.

When the story reaches its 'golden' state (a term I stole from my software development days), it and the rest of the issue's content is sent to our digital conversion programmer. She puts the PDF, ePub, and mobi files together. We provide these to the authors and several editors for one final proofread.

On publication day, the issue is posted on our website and made available for sale via our vendors.[10]

We take a day off. Then we start the process all over again. The needs of a periodical never cease.

All the reasons I enjoyed being an editor back in 2006 still apply today. The thrill of finding diamonds in your slush pile never fades. Those moments when you're able to humblebrag to your readers that a story you're publishing is the author's first professional sale feels really, really great. You can tell the world you've birthed a new writer.

---

[10] Jason always knew how to pick stories. I remember the first time I read an Apex story, I realized it was better than the entire last issue I'd read of a certain big-name big-shot publication that shall remain nameless (only because I dozed off while reading it and probably dreamed the whole thing). He was also stubborn... whether that was the redhead thing or the driving force of the aliens controlling him, I have no idea. So I kind of always figured the rest would fall into place for him and for Apex. Or at least it would if he could tame that hillbilly accent into pronouncing "horror" without it sounding like "whore." I think that was always his biggest challenge... especially after that border patrol incident on the way to Canada for a con. **(Deb Taber, first senior editor of Apex Publications)**

When you're an author and your story is one of three selected from our slush that month, you know you've accomplished something big. Approximately 0.33% of stories we receive are chosen for publication.

We at Apex like to think being published by us is a big deal. The machinations of publishing are slow, but when they're done, the results are beautiful.

After the release of a well-received and successful third issue of *Apex Science Fiction and Horror Digest*, an avalanche of momentum pushed the company forward. All the hard work and time I'd put in attending fandom conventions had spread the good word regarding my new press. Via networking, *Apex Digest* landed enough recognizable big name authors to help build our reputation in the writing community as a great place to publish. All the countless hours swimming through the slush pile had paid off with fantastic stories. Readers now sought us out for our quality, and writers wanted to work with us.

Although I started with the intention of building the best small press zine possible, I knew that in the long run I had grander designs. I had my eyes on the big prize: national distribution. Thanks to a referral by Alethea Kontis, I was able to land valuable phone time with an accounts manager at Ingram Periodicals. At the time, Ingram Periodicals was the second-largest distributor of magazines in the United States. They sourced everybody from discount grocery stores to big chain bookstores such as Barnes & Noble and Borders. Having a chance to make a personal connection with a manager at Ingram Periodicals was a huge opportunity, and I wasn't going to waste it.

The first call with the accounts manager went well. I turned my personal charm setting to 'Overflow' and added a dash of intellectual derring-do to the mix. The accounts manager seemed impressed with me and *Apex Digest*, and invited me to submit an application for distribution directly to her and her boss, therefore bypassing the first line of potential rejection.

Jumping the slush pile is a fantastic feeling!

By this point, issue 4 was out and issue 5 was going to press. We had landed some striking cover art by the artist Alex McVey for the fifth issue (the infamous 'fish baby' image). In addition, issues 4 and 5 featured some heavyweight names: Ben Bova, William F. Nolan, Neil Gaiman, Sherrilyn Kenyon, Tom Piccirilli, Eugie Foster, and JA Konrath, to name a few. The timing, it was perfect! I submitted our application.

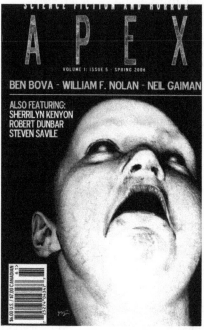

Cover art by Alex McVey

I had been warned that the wait time would be three to six months. I received an answer in six weeks.

They said "Yes!"

Wouldn't it be great if this story had a happy ending? I was heady with success, and despite not having gone to church in 15 years, I felt like the Big Man above was giving me a helpful shove.

Don't get me wrong, I have enough hubris to take all the credit.

I also have enough humility to accept that I made plenty of mistakes.

I don't dwell on the mistakes. Except in this book, of course... or lying in bed late at night.... Being an entrepreneur requires extraordinary leaps of a faith. It requires believing in your vision when nobody else will. You push through the failures to find the successes. And despite the mistakes and the less-than-happy ending, I consider *Apex Science Fiction and Horror Digest* to be a huge success.

Things moved quickly after *Apex Digest* had been accepted for distribution by Ingram. My sales rep ordered 3,000 copies of issue 5. This meant I needed to have 5,000 printed to cover our subscribers, comps, review copies, direct sales, etc. This also meant my printing costs would double. Due to a lack of foresight, I had not saved enough money to cover this (obvious) increase in printing cost required for distribution.

I walked the company into the Ingram distribution deal aware of *some* costs of doing business with them: chargebacks, returns, Net 270 payment structures, 55% to 60% discounts on retail to just name a few. I realized it would be a long, long time before I would be paid, and it would be an even longer amount of time before I would receive a sizable check.

I tried to take all of this into consideration and map out a budget for the coming 12 months. Releasing quarterly, I estimated I would be out of the red and rolling in the black in five to six issues (15 to 18 months). I just had to survive until then.

Apex would have to subsist on a diet of ramen noodles and supermarket-brand soda!

I took out a large bank loan to cover my costs for the next six months. To recuperate some of the money in the short term, I increased the retail price of each issue. Advertising prices also went up—a natural effect of greater visibility and circulation—and I decided to push harder for ad buys. As a result, Apex had income pouring in at record amounts, but we also had record expenses.

Rack sales (sales of a periodical in a brick and mortar store) of issue 5 were strong. We had a buy through rate of over 50% after 45 days. The buy through rate is the percentage of copies sold and not returned to the distributor. According to my analysis, our rate was 15 to 20% higher than average. Direct sales sold from the Apex website and at events remained strong despite the national availability of the magazine. My sales rep expressed great enthusiasm due to our numbers. The genre insiders noticed the new short fiction publication sitting next to the regular old guys: *Asimov's*, *F&SF*, and *Analog*. Emails from readers and authors letting me know that they had seen the digest out in the wild poured in. My answer to each was "Well, did you buy it???"

I would sit for hours or more at my local Barnes & Noble to stare at my *Apex Digest* sitting next to the usual suspects on the shelf. Through my Apex-colored goggles, I noticed how much newer, fresher, prettier *Apex Digest* looked compared to the others.

Desperate to make my buy through rates better, I would accost customers at the Lexington Joseph-Beth Booksellers and Barnes and Noble stores. Any fish that got near the bait (*Apex Digest*) would be rushed upon by my hard sale.

"Hey, did you know I edit and publish *Apex Science Fiction and Horror Digest* right here in Lexington?"

"Come on, put down that *F&SF* and try something different. Support a local guy!"

"I'll read you the story of your choice if you buy a copy."

The hard sell didn't work. It never works for me.

At one point, I met the B&N employee responsible for periodicals at the Lexington store. He gushed when he found out the new magazine came from a local publisher and placed a drop card under the magazine with the headline "Published in Lexington!"

Issue 6 featured cover art by Steven Gilberts, a fantastic horror and fantasy artist from near Louisville, KY. Once more, we had an eclectic mix of famous genre authors on the cover:

Ben Bova, Poppy Z. Brite, and Kage Baker. All the same, our Ingram sales rep placed a conservative order of 3,500 copies. I had 6,000 copies printed.

Our buy through rate hovered around 50% after 45 days. This was encouraging news. Both the sales rep and I had expected a sharp drop off. We surmised that issue 5 did so well because of its great cover, a solid table of contents, and most importantly, the appearance of a new fiction zine would pique the curiosity of genre readers. However, with issue 6 sales being strong, it appeared as if *Apex Digest* was retaining readers and had even gained some.

Around this time, I received the first inkling of what my Ingram payout would be for issue 5. Reports stated that 1,600 copies had sold via Ingram Periodicals. According to my math, Apex would receive a check for $800. That barely covered the cost of the fiction and artwork (our rate at the time was 1 cent a word). The amount of chargebacks Apex incurred was ridiculous. The distributor charged us for shipping our magazine to their warehouse. Apex was charged a warehouse fee for the short amount of time Ingram held the issue before shipping them to the store. There was a fee surcharge for handling per unit. Then every copy returned to Ingram by a store cost us the net price of the copy (expected, of course) along with a $0.40 processing fee and another $0.15 handling fee.

Reading this, I'm sure you're shaking your head and wondering if I had read the contract. It is a fair question, to be sure.

Of course, I read the contract. It was 25 pages of bafflegab on legal-sized paper, but I read every indecipherable word of it. Five times, at least. Some of the charges I expected. Others, based on my reading, were penalties that would kick in only in certain circumstances. I asked my sales rep and account manager many questions. They were forthright and honest as far as I could ascertain.

Know-it-alls will point out that I should have had a contract lawyer review the agreement with Ingram. Well, I *did*. Our lawyer said it all appeared copacetic.

Looking back, the problem wasn't that I didn't do my due diligence. It's that I did my due diligence incorrectly. Specifically, I didn't ask the right questions. I didn't seek out another periodical publisher and have a knowledge transfer regarding the pitfalls of distribution. The contract lawyer made sure that our agreement didn't contain any unethical terms and dangerous liability issues. But I failed to ask the lawyer how many ways could Ingram take money from Apex and the whys of such expenses. I knew going in how much Ingram charged for returns and that there were a lot of fees, but I never asked my account manager to give me a detailed breakdown or example accounting sheets.

I think about that youthful entrepreneur with his upstart publication and shake my head. If I could tell him a few key things, my life for many years after would have been so much easier.

Issue 7 rolled around, and by now my sales rep felt confident enough to push for an expansion. They ordered 5,000 copies. I had 8,000 printed.[11]

Sales tanked.

Issue 7 would be our worst-selling issue. Our sell through rate barely reached 30%, even after I made an 11th hour plea to Apex diehards to go out and buy copies. Even direct sales were down. I've had a lot of time to analyze what went wrong, and while I will never know for sure, I do have an idea. Most likely, the cover art did not connect with prospective buyers. It's bright orange. The image's focus is a naked woman in a fetal position surrounded by alien hands. The PG-13 rated nudity and placing a woman in a vulnerable position like that did not interest our progressive readers. Also, the

---

[11] I always had a weird sort of trust in Jason. Sometimes he'd get into trouble, but he was always very honest about it, and I always believed he'd work his way out. As a writer, you have to develop a quick intuition about the people you work with—we don't always get it right, God knows!—but I never doubted him. Of course, back then, *neither* of us had any idea what we were doing! Which is probably the best sort of way to go into writing and publishing, respectively…. **(Lavie Tidhar)**

cover lacked bankable names. Lavie Tidhar can headline a zine these days, but back in 2006, he was still a rising star.

With the poor payouts, rising print costs, and a looming miniscule payout, I recognized the fraying threads of my big dream.

Beginning with issue 8, I increased the cover price to $7.00 and bumped up the ad rates once more. I calculated that for Apex to break even we needed a sell through of 45% on a distribution of 8000 copies. Our subscriber base needed to reach 750. At those numbers, we would break even.

Issues 8 did okay, but we fell short of our sales goal. Issue 9 did great due to a Kevin J. Anderson novelette and some jaw-dropping artwork by Paul Bielaczyc. But the zine was wobbling financially.

In one last desperate measure, I trimmed the page count to save a few grand on printing costs. Issue 10 almost broke even. Our debt continued to mount thanks to finance charges and making minimum payments.

As production for issue 11 completed, I realized the end was near. Issue 12 would be the last one.

I would go out kicking and screaming. So I decided Issue 12 would be a grand double issue. We finally landed a coveted Brian Keene story. Hal Duncan sold us an interview with rising star Jeff Vander-Meer. The cover art featured a guy wearing embedded lenses looking skyward. I imagined the guy was a dreamer. Like me.

Apex Science Fiction and Horror Digest, volume 1, issue 12 was the last one. I cancelled our distribution agreement with Ingram Periodicals. This chapter of my publishing career came to a sputtering halt. With that last issue we had reached our circulation goal of 8,000 and had a subscriber base of 750. But it was a case of too little, too late.

I learned a great many things in the two years I worked with

Ingram Periodicals and five smaller companies that distributed *Apex Digest*.

1) The magazine distribution business is designed in such a manner that you cannot succeed unless you have a readership that numbers in the tens of thousands. Your ad revenue has to be your primary source of income. Newsstand sales aren't a viable source of revenue for smaller publications. I learned lesson 1 the hard way.

2) Barring a circulation of tens of thousands, you'll need hundreds of thousands of dollars to reach that circulation goal.

3) Rookie publishers should never try to jump into the national distribution hot pot.

4) When all was said and done, I was $70,000 in debt to my printer, to my bank, and to my credit cards.

I've read that many entrepreneurs create a chain of bankrupt businesses in the course of finding one that makes them wealthy and famous. All the same, I did not want to go down the path of bankruptcy. I owed the money, and I would pay it back. It might take me years, but I would do it, and I would do it using Apex funds.

Also, most people outside the Apex circle, by all appearances, saw *Apex Digest* as a smashing success. How could I let such social equity go to waste?

No, I wouldn't let the opportunity pass. I wasn't done with publishing. It wasn't time to go bankrupt. It *was* time to change the Apex Publications business focus.

The digest would be reincarnated as an online publication. The rest of the company would expand into books and eBooks.

By 2007 and 2008, the eBook tsunami would be crashing on the beaches of the publishing business. I could see it approaching on the horizon, and I wanted to be surfing that magnificent wave of money when it hit.

NOTE:

**Dear Mr. Sizemore, I don't
write for free. But, as a personal favor
to you, I will edit this for the duration of me
sitting on the toilet. — Maurice Broaddus**

I t takes a special person to throw an event in his or her
own honor. Maurice Broaddus is just that special person. It makes *sense* that Maurice Broaddus would host a convention named Mo*Con (short for Maurice Convention).

FAITH

GENDER

RACE

HORROR

MO CON VI

RETURN OF THE KING

Maurice also appears as the hero in posters
for Mo*Con (Poster credit Bob Freeman).

I've known Maurice for almost as long as I've been running Apex Publications. **(As a brief aside, we formally met at Conglomeration in 2006. I made the trip to the convention specifically to meet Mr. Sizemore as well as visit the wondrous Alethea Kontis. Thinking back, this may have been one of the most pivotal cons in my career, as I made two friends I've held close for nearly a decade. That said, I still remember the fateful conversation where you pointed out that "You did a con named after yourself, despite having no credits, and people actually showed up. That's someone Apex needs to get in bed with." I'm sure there will come a point where I'll be bringing this up in my eventual sexual harassment lawsuit against you.)** In that time I've learned a good many things about the man. When he grows out his beard he bears an uncanny resemblance to Laurence Fishburne. He likes his wine sweet and his food spicy. And unlike most people in the business of publishing, he derives strength and energy from socializing. The more friends he can make, the more people he can talk to in any one place, the happier Maurice is going to be.

He used to call himself the Sinister Minister. Though I can tell you he's not particularly sinister. In fact I've never been convinced that he has ever been an ordained minister. But he loves the attention the same way a doomsday preacher sermonizing on a street corner does. **(To be fair, I was given the nom-de-guerre Sinister Minister by fellow writer, Brian Knight. Point of fact, he and I share the same birthday. Another point of fact, perhaps the "sinister" part of that description explains why I've been kicked out of so many churches.)**

Mo*Con isn't your typical fandom convention. For starters, it is almost always held in the basement of a Baptist church in Indianapolis. **(Speaking of being kicked out, in the history of Mo*Con, we've gone through three churches. The Methodists, however, love us.)** For some of the attendees, this is the only time each year he or she will step into the den of God. Only three panels are organized, with one panel being a relevant and current hot button social issue. One year it was "Homosexuality and the Church." Another was "Writing About Sex and Horror." Many nervous jokes are made about lightning or a tornado striking, sending the whole place tumbling down on our heads.

Thankfully, the Good Lord has chilled a bit since the Old Testament times!

The convention feeds its attendees Friday night, Saturday afternoon, and Sunday morning. And I'm not talking boring convention staples of bagels and finger cheese. **(Which isn't to say that we don't have cheese. Ambassador to all races that I am, I have it on pretty good authority that white people love their cheese.)** Attendees are treated to feasts of Indian cuisine, Jamaican cuisine, and homemade bacon, eggs, and pancakes. Gluttony is a favorite sin of Maurice's, and we're lucky that he likes to share it.

From a socializing and networking standpoint, the Saturday night house party is the highlight of the weekend. Everyone converges on the Broaddus homestead (I've never understood how he convinces his wife, Sally, to let this happen every year) to partake in leftovers, fellowship, and alcohol. Granted, this party has paid dividends to Maurice and his writing career. **(My wife, who is both white and a lover of cheese, once asked me "What exactly goes on at a writer's convention?" Thus the Mo*Con pre-party was born with the first Mo*Con. Back then, Mo*Con was on Sunday, which gave us the excuse to party on Saturday night. The next morning she said that it looked like a bomb went off at a writer's convention judging from how many bodies she had to step over Sunday morning.)**

There's an old adage that states the best way to find freelance work or make book deals is to hang out at the bar of the convention's host hotel. That's because publishers and editors are, for the most part, heavy drinkers. You can guess the myriad reasons this is true, but I'll leave them unsaid for the purpose of plausible deniability. **(What do you call a gathering of writers? A BAR! Besides, I'm used to spending long hours alone in front of a keyboard. And have many social phobias. Plus a side of me that leans toward the introverted. Naturally I drink to be able to be around other people. But that's just me. I'm sure no other writer is like that.)**

I've long suspected that Mo*Con is actually Maurice's personal Bar Con. **(I'm putting this on our next flyer.)**

For example, the second (or perhaps the third... these things have started to run all together on me) Mo*Con I attended is where the idea of *Dark Faith* originated. Scratch that. It is where the agreement to *publish* the anthology that would become *Dark Faith* occurred. What is *Dark Faith*? It's a dark fantasy and horror anthology edited by Maurice Broaddus and Jerry Gordon, themed around the concept of faith, be it faith in religion, others, or yourself.

Maurice had pitched me the idea earlier that weekend: a collection of stories by past and present Mo*Con attendees around the concept of faith. He tossed out the names of potential contributors: Brian Keene, Tom Piccirilli, Wrath James White, Chesya Burke, Alethea Kontis, and so on. The project sounded awesome. I wanted to do the project, but Maurice and I knew we had to pay the authors a pro rate (5 cents a word) to make it happen, and that made *Dark Faith* too expensive for me to seriously consider. This was before the advent of Kickstarter and the rise of crowdfunding. Apex would have had to eat the cost of production and authors and editors and designers and artists. Anthologies are typically low-sellers, so such an anthology would never clear the red.

I was disappointed. Maurice was disappointed. But disappointment is common in the world of publishing, so I didn't stay heartbroken for too long. If I'm being generous, I'll say fifteen minutes.

The weekend continued on. Nick Mamatas performed feats of strength which included lifting me over his head using his hip. This was no small miracle, as I was a hefty 260 pounds back then. A Celtic band wore kilts and played for what felt like sixteen hours. Steven Gilberts headlined an art show. A nice fellow named John Hay wove entertaining stories while he knitted. **(Luckily, Jason skipped the "how one of our Mo*Con guests of honor almost go arrested" incident.)**

And as it turned out John Hay **(Point of fact: John Hay also shares his birthday with me and Brian Knight)** had a secret friend: the green fairy.

The other attendees and I had convened at Maurice's house for the Mo*Con party throw down that Saturday night. I started out innocently enough with a beer or two. My hope was to drink lightly and get up early the next day, so I would be able to get home before dark to get some chores finished before the weekend ended.

Outside the Broaddus's garage, John had set up shop with his knitting. He regaled his friends with poetry and amusing life anecdotes. In front of him was a low table and on this table rested a fancy glass and silver decanter that dripped an unknown fluid from dual spigots into two cups covered with a spoon, filter and a sugar cube. Being young and naïve, I had never seen such a contraption before. Now I know it as a glass absinthe fountain.

(I'm going to stop Jason right here. You'd think we'd have known better. Earlier that year, my local writers group, the Indiana Horror Writers, had a retreat. We'd had absinthe there. Coincidentally, John Hay was there also, but I believe the absinthe fairy this time was Mr. Douglas F. Warrick. I have exactly two memories from after the bottle was opened: at some point I sang "The Lion Sleeps Tonight" during karaoke and someone was demonstrating the sign language for strippers. This is also referred to as "The IHW retreat no one remembers.")

I walked over and spoke to John.

"Hey, man, what do you have going on here?" I motioned to the fountain.

"Young fellow," John said, "have you ever partaken of the green fairy?"

I had no clue what he meant by the green fairy. "Um, no?"

"Come closer, friend, come closer." He directed me to a chair across from him, placing the fountain between us.

"This is a traditional absinthe fountain. It is a choice way to serve this particular and compelling aperitif. Fountains just like this could be found in all the upscale bars of 19th century Parisian cafes." **(FTR, John loves using words like "aperitif." I often refer to him as my fancy friend.)**

"Oh. I see." I pointed at the two spigots. "Why the two nozzles?"

"Ah, Mr. Sizemore, the green fairy is best prepared carefully and slowly to appreciate its full potential. Simply fill the fountain with iced water, place your glass of absinthe below the spigot with a single sugar cube placed over a slotted spoon and adjust the tap to your desired flow. The cold water will gradually dissolve the sugar and mix with the absinthe in a process known as louching." **(Louching. I told you: fancy.)**

I peered closer. "How does it taste?"

A wide grin appeared across John's face. "Intoxicating." **(This is John speak for "I dare you to put this in your mouth.")**

"Can I have some?"

"Of course, the cup to your left is ready. Just switch off the spigot and place the spoon on the napkin and the serving is yours."

"Great, thanks!"

"Mr. Sizemore, an imperative bit of advice—"

I never heard John's important words of wisdom, because I threw back the cup of absinthe without abandon and drank it down. The absinthe tasted like black licorice, a flavor I abhor. **(Licorice shit out by a squirrel.)**

John read my face. "That is the anise, which is what most people think black licorice tastes like."

The sweetness of the drink made my teeth ache. "Isn't there any alcohol in it?"

"Oh, yes, yes. Had you sipped the absinthe like the fine gentleman you are, perhaps you would have savored the rolling flavors of the alcohol over the bite of the anise."

I felt let down. Like I had messed up. I wanted to do this properly. I asked John if I could try a second cup of absinthe, and this time, I promised, I would sip it like a gentleman. I saw John look over to a group of people talking with Maurice. Maurice looked up and he and John made the briefest of eye contact.

"Well... I was preparing the other cup for Mr. Broaddus, but I do not think he will mind waiting a while longer so that his fine guest can enjoy the green fairy in all her beauty."

I took the second cup. I started sipping.

(Okay, okay, okay. Where was this exchange?

Jason: Why so little? Is this just to sample it?

John: No, this is your whole evening's worth of absinthe. Trust me.

Jason: Aw man, pour it like you mean it.)

I have no further memories of that Saturday night. To this day, it troubles me that hours of my life simply disappeared. It is similar to what happens when you're put under for general anesthesia, except with general anesthesia you have vaguely remembered dreams. There are no dreams or memories of that evening. Everything is black. And missing.

The next day I woke up in the bed of Maurice's oldest son. How I got there, I do not know. The scent of bacon pulled me from the last remnants of sleep and I rejoined the world of the lucid.

As I stepped into the living room, Jerry Gordon approached me. He was holding a plate of steaming eggs and fresh bacon. Jerry was smiling. He took my hand and shook it, telling me he can't wait to get to work on the book we're doing together. I kind of mumbled an agreement, shook my head, and ventured off in search of Maurice.

I found our hardworking **(You have no idea. Oh, Lord Jesus, the cups. THE CUPS! We found cups in places we didn't know were rooms. Seriously, who did absinthe in my bedroom closet?)** convention host holding court in the living room with a group of young writers. Maurice was lecturing them on the evils of working "for exposure." **(I told you, I don't work for free. Exposure can't buy my groceries. Exposure can't pay my light bill. But exposure can nearly get you arrested, but that was a different con.)** When he saw me, he excused himself, walked over, and hugged me.

"Hey, good morning, Mr. Apex!" he greeted.

"Good morning."

"John Hays tells me you danced with the green fairy last night."

I sighed, embarrassed. "Yeah... I don't remember much of anything after my second cup of absinthe."

Maurice looked stricken. "What do you mean you don't remember? We had a lengthy discussion about the direction of Apex and the *Dark Faith* anthology."

Uh oh, I thought.

"We did?"

"We did. I wrote it all down." Maurice grabbed a yellow pad off the coffee table. "See, you even left some notes." **(In sales, we refer to this as "the assumptive close.")**

I looked. My comments and notes were all over the damn thing.

"So, listen. We've locked up Brian Keene for the anthology. This is going to be a big deal. Best anthology you've published."

I received another hug. My stomached ached, not from the expected hangover, but for what I had gotten myself into.

Dark Faith did turn into a fantastic anthology. Maurice and

Jerry put together a roster of talented authors and a book filled with amazing short fiction and poetry. The book earned a Stoker Award nomination. Jennifer Pelland's story "Ghosts of New York" made me cry and earned a Nebula Award nomination. Catherynne M. Valente's story "The Days of Flaming Motorcycles" was a WSFA nominee. Four different stories were reprinted in the various annual Year's Best anthologies. It's a book I'm proud of.

But the expense of producing *Dark Faith* nearly caused Apex to go bankrupt. We went over our targeted word count. We paid everybody pro rates. We had the book traditionally printed (the only Apex title done so). We had *way* too many copies made. Apex is still in the red for the Dark Faith project. **("We" did this. Perhaps if "we" didn't begin our marketing meetings by asking me what I'm drinking, or worse, drinking enough of it to find out why a drink is actually NAMED *Hypnotiq*, "we" wouldn't have had such problems. To be fair, I probably could have stopped some of his mad planning, but I never get in the way of an angry redhead yelling things like "What's MY name?" and "Why can't I feel my tongue?")**

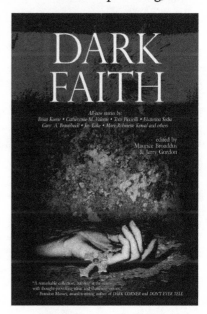

To be fair, *Dark Faith* has sold well. Very well. But I also give away boxes and copies to charity and convention swag bags at every opportunity. And even with doing that, I still have 600+ copies taking up a copious space in my garage.

I hope to never see absinthe again.

Cover art by Edith Walter

Too many of my successes have spun out of personal failures and an inability to pump the brakes on bad decisions: *Dark Faith*, magazine distribution, book distribution, and convention adventures I include among these failures. Despite making mistakes hand over fist, I feel like I've managed to spin these failed experiences into an overall net positive. The business, after a decade, still exists, and is doing quite well. You might credit this to an incredible streak of lucky ineptitude. However, I prefer to market the process as my alternative pathways to superior business acumen.[12]

After the debacle of national periodical distribution had left me in debt, morose, and eager to move on to the next chapter of my life, an exciting change in the publishing business was occurring. Print on demand technology was changing the business paradigm of the printed word. I simply could not pass this up without dipping my entrepreneurial toes into the stream. I decided that I needed to cleanse my publishing palate with a book—an anthology of horror written by a group of authors whom I would hand select. Any genre person knows that if

---

[12] The secret to Apex's success is not a deal with the devil, or even the sort of charisma that attracts people willing to walk around in public with an offer of extraterrestrial fellatio emblazoned across their torsos. It's that, no matter what changes happen in the publishing industry, Jason simply refuses to let Apex go. It might be the epic levels of stubbornness of a ginger hillbilly. Frankly, I think it is because if Apex fails to thrive, Jason would need to start over with a more traditional midlife crisis. I've seen his garage; he has too many back issues of *Apex Digest* and *Dark Faith* to fit a sports car in there. **(Janet Harriett)**

there's one surefire method for an amateur editor to make a name for himself in the publishing world, it's by self-publishing a print-on-demand horror anthology.

So here we go again. I had decided to do a project that had a low probability of making money. Many self-published horror anthologies are produced, and many are roundly and rightly mocked: ugly covers, poorly edited stories, authors paid with "exposure," crappy titles.

But after three years, I felt wise and smart enough to avoid the downfalls that plague so many self-published horror anthologies, and I was determined I would not allow my anthology to wear any of those labels. My first act would be to give my book a clever and fancy pants Latin name: *Aegri Somnia* (meaning "a sick man's dream").

Aegri Somnia is a terrible title.

From a marketing perspective, there are several reasons why this is not a good title.

1) Most people will not know how to pronounce it. To compound matters, due to my accent, I have problems pronouncing it properly.

2) Most people will not know how to spell it.

3) It is not a name that is easy to remember.

4) It sounds pretentious.

As you can see, I started my first book project on the right track.

To my credit, I did pay the anthology authors a whopping penny a word. This was certainly not a rate any of them deserved (the professional rate back in 2007 was five cents a word), but I rationalized that it was a penny a word more than writing for exposure.

The cover, while not the best that Apex Publications has pushed out to the world, was serviceable. For the artwork, I had called on Michael Bielaczyc (a wonderful fellow who I had met at the infamous Ham Hypericon) to create a visual interpretation of "a sick man's dream." The artwork is beautiful. I've seen it displayed at shows. The piece is large and vibrant and complicated. But on the front of a book, it does not give readers any sense of what they're holding in their hands. This cover fail should not be placed at the feet of Michael Bielaczyc. Instead, blame me. I did a terrible job explaining to Michael my vision.

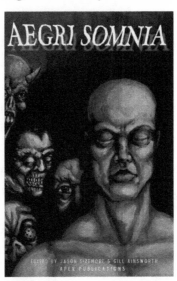

Cover art by Michael Bielaczyc

The saving grace that spared *Aegri Somnia* from becoming just another crappy horror anthology was my eye for finding talented, relatively unknown writers. The table of contents read like this: Scott Nicholson, Cherie Priest, Christopher Rowe, Steven Savile, Lavie Tidhar, Jennifer Pelland, Eugie Foster, Nancy Fulda, Mari Adkins, Angeline Hawkes, Rhonda Eudaly, and Bryn Sparks. They were invited to write to the theme of aegri somnia and they knocked it out of the park.

My co-editor Gill Ainsworth and I were nominated for the Bram Stoker Award for Superior Achievement in an Anthology. To this day, I consider this a most impressive accomplishment.

The award nomination proved to be a wonderful blessing and a terrible curse.

I came down with an incurable case of book fever. I went from relationship rebound to obsessed practically overnight.

Apex Publications gained immediate acclaim in genre circles. The Stokers have a level of prestige rivaling its big brothers and sisters — the Hugo Award, Nebula Award, and World Fantasy Award — so make no mistake, it is a big deal to be nominated. The Stoker Award also presents the coolest looking trophy of any literary award: a beautifully designed haunted house with a front door that opens to reveal a brass plaque engraved with your name and award.

The year that *Aegri Somnia* was nominated, the Stoker Awards were presented at the World Horror Convention held in Toronto. Toronto is an eleven-hour drive from Lexington, so flying would have been the smart choice, but two close friends who shall remain anonymous offered to ride north with me and share the driving duties. Splitting gas and a hotel room between three people would save a lot of money for an expensive trip. They were dating and I loathed being a third wheel, but saving money was paramount at the time.

After an uneventful drive into Canada, we arrived Friday night at our hotel. Our room could best be described as a large closet. One twin sized bed took half the available floor space. The front of the bed pressed against a large oak dresser. Looking around, I had no idea how three people could possibly sleep in this place. The plan had been for two of us to sleep in the bed and one on the floor, but that obviously wasn't going to work. I'm not a huge guy, but I am big enough to take up most of a twin bed.

I rushed downstairs to the registration area and accosted the nice Canadian behind the desk. His name badge read "John."

"Hi, John. Can I get another room?"

He stared at me as if I was speaking in tongues. "Excuse me?"

I stared back. After a moment, I realized my accent had thrown him off. I took a deep breath, mentally trying to clean up my rolling vowels and contractions before asking again.

"Is there something wrong with your room?"

"Yes. It's too small. I need a bigger room." I gave him my room number.

"Bigger?" John pecked on the keyboard of his station terminal. "I'm sorry, sir, all our rooms are that size."

I raised an eyebrow. "If all the rooms are the same size, why were you typing?"

John leaned in, casting an ear in my direction. "Excuse me?"

I repeated the question.

"I'm sorry. I don't understand what you're saying."

"Bite me."

John looked aghast. "Is that necessary?"

I gritted my teeth. "Oh, you understand me now?"

Again, John leaned in. "Excuse me?"

I resist the urge to scream. "Can I get a foldout bed?"

"A portable bed?"

"Yes!"

"Let me check." He pecked at the keyboard again.

Back in the room, after the bed had been delivered, my friends and I struggled to maneuver our bodies in a way so we would have room to unfold the portable and still have a place to stand. We twisted and turned, pulling at the foldout bed from all angles and smacking into the walls the entire time. At one point I was standing on the twin bed, shouting directions. The whole situation would have played well in a Three Stooges film. Eventually we got the bed unfolded; it fit snugly between the twin bed and wall. Dripping with sweat, we stared at our accomplishment, but we didn't feel pride or satisfaction. Instead a deep sense of trepidation hung in the air. The three of us would share that tiny space.

The Stoker Awards were scheduled for Saturday night. I put on my ill-fitting suit and tie and found Gill Ainsworth waiting outside in the hall. Unlike me, she looked stunning. Together we walked into the banquet hall and took a seat at our pre-arranged place. According to a small placard on the table, the pre-awards banquet menu had three options: pork, seafood, and vegetarian. I'm no fan of seafood. Vegetarian invariably left me hungry, and I didn't want my stomach growling through the entire award ceremony. The waiter gave me a baleful stare while standing impatient and curt as I agonized over my choices. I made the fateful decision of pork.

Jason Sizemore & Gill Ainsworth pre-Stoker Awards

Dinner ordered, the host staff rolled out carts of beer and wine and bread and cheese. Gill and I clinked glasses and started imbibing. Before the food arrived, we finished off a bottle of vino and worked on a second. The food tasted okay—typical banquet quality—so I wolfed it down. I needed it to sop up some of the wine sloshing around my belly. The last thing I wanted to do was stumble drunkenly to the podium in the odd chance that Gill and I won.

About 30 minutes after the entrees arrived, the award ceremony started. As more and more people accepted their cool little haunted houses for winning, my stomach gurgled more and more in agitation. I wrote it off as nerves. Waiting for your category to be announced is a nerve-wracking job. Nerves or not, however, the building urge to hurl made me uncomfortable.

Finally, the Superior Achievement in an Anthology category was announced. They named off the nominees. I heard "*Aegri Somnia*, edited by Jason Sizemore and Gill Ainsworth."

Friends at our table and around us cheered and clapped.

And the winner is....

Well... it wasn't Gill and me. My stomach spit acid up my esophagus. I politely applauded and listened quietly as the winner gave their acceptance speech. The second they finished, I rushed off, not even excusing myself, for the bathroom where I lost my breakfast, lunch, and dinner.

Afterward, I tried to mingle. Usually, post-purge, you'll feel much better for a little while. Not this time.

- "Jason, you look deathly. Don't be so down, you'll get nominated again one day."
- "Jason, do you ever climb out of your Apex cave? You look like the monsters in *The Descent.*"
- "Jason, I thought albinos had white hair?"

I got it. I looked sick. I'd had enough, so I stumbled my way back to the hotel and fell face first unto our mutant bed and went straight to sleep.

The next morning, I felt worse. My two roommates were piled on top of me. One snored directly in my face. The other had a puddle of drool inching dangerously close to my face. The smell of saliva made my internals lurch. I bounced up and made it by a fraction of a second to the toilet before my stomach turned itself inside out and evacuated all contents.

My roommates woke up to the sound of me barfing.

"Dude, are you sick?"

"Shit, man, why didn't you tell us you were sick before we slept in a puppy pile?"

I didn't have the energy to explain myself. I felt certain I had food poisoning. Dragging myself back to the bed, I dropped back down and emitted a pitiful, zombie-like groan. Merciful sleep took me again.

Several hours later, a loud argument between my roommates jarred me awake. Somebody had seen something someone shouldn't have seen, creating major problems. One left, slamming the door in his wake. The other stayed. Sitting up, I did my best to comfort and be a friend, but my body shook and I felt my stomach convulsing. Sleep beckoned, wishing to shut me down while whatever ate at me either worked its way out of my body or put me out of my misery.

I think I fainted, because the next thing I remember it was 4 a.m. and my roommates were puppy piled on me again. I climbed out of bed and got a drink of water from the bathroom tap, staring at the clock with dread. In the morning, we would have to leave before 11 a.m.

Once everyone woke up, we discussed our options. I brought up the possibility of staying another night in the hopes I would improve enough to be upright for the drive back. This was shot down because one roommate had to report to work the next day. In the end, we decided to leave, and I would drive as much as my body would allow. Since one roommate didn't have a drivers permit, the driving would be left to two of us.

Due to my illness, my roommate with the driver's license took the wheel first. After an hour, she suddenly stopped.

"What is it?" I asked.

"I'm getting a migraine." She had both palms pressed to her eyes, head leaning forward onto the steering wheel. "A bad one."

"You need me to drive?"

"Yes, please."

She crawled onto the bench seat in the back of my truck and covered her face with her jacket. I felt bad for her. The pain must have been excruciating for her to stop when she knew I was sick. Myself, I barely had the energy to take my place behind the steering wheel.

We were ten hours from home.

As the miles crept by, my other driver got worse. When her vision blurred, it became clear she would not be driving any further that day.

I focused on staying awake and alert. My body fought me.

Several times I had to pull over to dry heave, crying over the agony racking my body.

Those ten hours are among the most miserable I've ever been through.

And I didn't even win the damn Stoker.

Fast forward three years, and Apex Publications had built up an impressive catalog of titles. Most of the authors I had met via my travels to conferences and conventions, or I had worked with them through the magazine. Our first collection, *Unwelcome Bodies*, is by Jennifer Pelland, who is probably our readers' favorite author from *Apex Digest*. Another collection, *Taste of Tenderloin* by Gene O'Neill, won a Stoker Award, while Fran Friel's *Mama's Boy and Other Dark Tales* earned a Stoker nomination. Gary A. Braunbeck's nonfiction book *To Each Their Darkness* also won a Stoker. I met all three of these authors via the friendships I had made at Hypericon and the World Horror Convention when I attended the Stoker Award ceremony.

With my inventory of critically-praised books, once more, I felt the call to expand the business.[13] I sought out national distribution. Again, I had a friend with all the right connections who knew all the right people to call, so I landed a deal with Diamond Book Distribution, the little brother to their monolithic comic distributor, in a matter of weeks. A few days later, I received our first purchase order from Diamond that nearly knocked me out of my seat. They needed several thousand copies of seven of our titles, which was way, way beyond my little company's financial capacity to produce. During this time, Apex bore a $50,000 debt like a rancid albatross around its neck, making the prospect of landing a sizable, unsecured small business loan impossible. The money in the company's piggy bank fell way short of covering potential printing costs.

While feeling disappointed and defeated at the time,

---

[13] Shouldn't I have learned to ignore this call by now? **(Jason Sizemore)**

this financial shortcoming probably saved the company and my sanity. I didn't have the resources to run a nationally distributed book company. Nor did I have the money to hire the people I would need.

Embarrassed and contrite, I explained to my Diamond rep that Apex would be unable to provide the titles and would have to backpedal out of our contract. Diamond took it in stride, and even extended an open invitation to have Apex back when we were in stronger position.

I still wanted distribution, but on a scale Apex could afford. I found a small company based out of Vermont that distributed to independent bookstores and specialty shops, like the bong and book store down the street from my day job office. The distributor agreed to take most of our titles. At the time, I felt good about the deal.

After a good start, things turned sour almost immediately. Personalities clashed. There was a major issue of mistrust. My plans of global domination were being usurped again.

My plan was a simple one: stair-step the company from a smaller customer base to larger. After five to ten years, Apex would have its debts paid and enough money in the bank to dance back into the arms of Diamond.

After I received our first quarterly sales report, I noticed some discrepancies. The wife of the husband/wife team who ran the company insisted that the data was correct. I explained to her that the reports were not showing sales of our books to certain bookstores. I was certain about this because a bookstore in Lexington sold me a copy of *Dark Faith* that they had obtained from my distributor. Since this data determined how much Apex was to be paid and that the error leaned heavily in favor of the distributor (of course), I was determined to see it corrected.

I really tried not to be 'that guy'. I wanted to be firm, but not pushy, regarding the issue. I called my rep a number of times asking to speak with their IT person. Eventually, I discovered that the IT person was the wife of the husband/wife team and that she created the reports in Microsoft Access. I requested she send me her Access database with the reports and non-Apex data deleted. She refused, most likely because she didn't know how to do that.

She grew hostile, like a honey badger protecting its kill. I accused them of stealing and lying. She responded by calling me a "retarded hillbilly twit." The conversation ended with me hanging up on her. An hour after our confrontation, she called and apologized. Likewise, I apologized. All I wanted was for the issue to be resolved. I want to make money, not war, after all.

The next day at 8 a.m. sharp, my cell phone chirped: a call from Vermont. My hopes soared. Maybe, just maybe, a solution was found.

It was the husband calling.

I picked up. "Hi," I said cheerfully, "I'm glad you've—"

"You're going to shut your fucking mouth and listen to what I say." The command caught me off guard. He sounded like R. Lee Ermey's sadistic drill sergeant in *Full Metal Jacket*. I shut my mouth and listened.

"If you ever talk to my wife again, I will drive down to Kentucky and shove a half-a-dozen of your awful books far up your ass. If you accuse us of cheating and lying to anyone, I will have my lawyers on you and have you put down like the rabid mutt you are. *We. Are. Done.* You understand that?"

"When do I get my last check?" I asked, unperturbed.

Click.

And just like that, my experience with book distribution ended.

It would take two years for Apex to recover the inventory that the distribution company held in their warehouse. Apex received less than half the money they owed me based on their versions of the sales report.

A few years ago, I stumbled upon a news blurb that explained what had happened to the company. It certainly makes me feel no better about my experience with them, though I now realize Apex was lucky to have recovered anything from the ordeal.

Soon after I received the fateful phone call from the husband, the company went Chapter 11. Obviously, if I had known of their financial woes, I could have avoided yet another problematic business decision.

There's a tragic footnote to this story. The husband died of lung cancer only months after the bankruptcy. I can't imagine the kind of stress the husband and wife were already dealing with when they signed Apex.

After two horrible experiences with traditional distribution, I elected to stay within my comfort zone: print-on-demand (POD) produced physical books and the surging eBook business. Although POD is well known in publishing circles, it is still a relatively unknown technology to many, so I'll briefly explain the difference between the POD business model and the traditional publishing model.

When most people think of publishing, they picture brick and mortar retailers such as Barnes & Noble and Walmart with racks of books available for browsing and perusal by the customer. What they don't realize is that a great majority of these books are published by the Big Five: Penguin Random House, Macmillan, HarperCollins, Hachette, and Simon & Schuster. If none of these names appear on the spine of a book in Barnes & Noble, then there is a good chance the book was published by one of their multitudes of publishing divisions. I will note that some larger independent presses do get distribution into the brick and mortars, but on the whole, if you can't buy cap space you're not going to sell a lot of books.

To provide copies to all the stores, tens of thousands of copies are printed of most Big Five books. Even at these numbers, the cost per unit of a 300-page trade paperback will be several dollars. Factor in the archaic practice of the returns system for bookselling, and small publishers are unable to handle the financial burdens of printing, producing, and marketing a nationally released book. Even now, I have 700 copies of *Dark*

Faith that have been sitting in my garage for seven years. But that's nothing. I've heard horror stories of writers and publishers with thousands of copies of their books lining the walls of their garages, their offices, and even bedrooms.

In the early 2000s, print-on-demand technology improved enough to make books of high enough quality so that potential buyers would not be turned off. Until this point, small press companies had to rely upon expensive low print runs of traditionally printed books. When this changed, the publishing industry witnessed a surge of new small press companies and the rise of self-publishing. Along with this a miracle occurred: the number of editors in the world quadrupled, as anybody with a few bucks and a few stories could throw an anthology together and call themselves 'editor'. I do the same thing when I go into the kitchen and boil some noodles. In the kitchen I am known as Chef Sizemore.

With POD technology, a publisher can order digitally printed books in single or multiple copies at a relatively low cost. Where before it might cost a press $1,200 to have 100 copies of a 300-page book printed, it now might cost $400 for those same books.

Additionally, some POD printers (such as Lightning Source and Createspace) are able to have your title placed in the various distribution catalogs such as Ingram and Baker & Taylor. This is a major plus, because bookstores, both online and brick and mortar, use these catalogs to place and fulfill orders at wholesale rates.

The combination of lower cost printing and access to the distribution catalogs makes it possible for small presses like Apex Publications to exist. Thanks to the miracles of technology, Apex and others of its ilk can bring you the work of fantastic authors who, for one reason or another, did not land a book deal with one of the Big Five.

Yet this is only half the story. The second side of the POD business model that Apex and most others branches into are eBooks. The technology of eBooks has been around for decades, but it really took off with the release of Amazon's Kindle hardware. Readers loved getting books that cost a fraction of the printed edition, and publishers loved making money without the headaches of distribution. A wave of money hit the publishing business. Then smart phones and tablets flooded the marketplace, and another wave of money hit the industry.

Apex was ready with its surfboard and jumped on the money wave head-on. The company was well-positioned to take advantage of POD and eBooks. I often lament my decision to become a software developer because I have difficulty succeeding in corporate environments. But the skills I possess because of the occupation have been crucial in the success of Apex Publications and *Apex Digest*. It gave me an early sense of where eBooks were heading, and *Apex Digest* was one of the few zines at the time that sold an eBook edition. I have saved tens of thousands of dollars by creating our digital products, creating and installing our websites and cart systems, and picking up the intricacies of accounting and publication software.

Apex has thrived under the non-traditional (though, these days, common) POD and digital business model. Although the cost of entry is lower, successful small presses are not as common as you might imagine. You must have a flexible and broad skillset that covers the spectrum of a liberal arts education: accounting, business management, fine arts, critical theory, psychology, math, interpersonal skills, and more. You can't do it alone, simply because there is too much for one person to do. If you're not sitting on a pot of gold, you're going to need help and be resourceful. For ten years, I've run Apex while maintaining a day job and raising two kids (and many other small press owners have to juggle a similar life). On occasion, you will need to ask a writer or artist friend for a favor, to work 'for exposure'.[14] Apex would be nowhere without the generosity of creative minds and patient friends. If and when your company becomes profitable, you pay that generosity forward. You hire your talented, patient artist and writer friends for any paying work you can. You take the time to work for exposure for others. Don't abuse karma. She always wins in the end.

---

[14] The creative community will go to great lengths to lend a hand when they can. This "gives back" culture is non-existent in the software development community I've worked in for the last 20 years. **(Jason Sizemore)**

Legend building: the act of performing grand and fantastic deeds in order to enhance one's reputation.

Maurice Broaddus explained to me during one of our late night discussions that the secret to legend building is that you don't have to perform the grand and fantastic deeds; people just need to believe that you do.

We were relaxing together on Maurice's loveseat, each sipping a fancy fruity cocktail. Maurice was holding court from his customary spot where the cushion sits three inches lower to the floor than the other. Maurice isn't obese; it's just that he does *a lot* of pontificating.

"That sounds disturbingly close to propaganda," I mumbled.

"Adjust your worldview," he said. "You're in the business of selling fiction, so start acting like it! This isn't the hills of Kentucky where you go around like a door-to-door Bible salesman."

"And that sounds disturbingly close to a stereotype," I mumbled.

Maurice gave me one of his withering *Seriously, dude?* stares. "You know what I mean."

I nodded. Of course I did.

"You have the prestige," he pointed out.

I nodded. I had enough prestige to feed every starving literary critic in the business!

"You have the books."

I nodded. Absolutely. Shelves and shelves of them on racks in my garage. Gathering dust.

"All you need are the readers."

And he lost me. I scratched my head, confused. "And you're going to tell me how I'm going to get more readers?"

"You need people talking about you. Talking about Apex. You need to build a legend around the Sizemore and Apex brand."

"Oh, so I need to go and start an internet flame war with Stephen King?"

"Good idea," Maurice said, "but, no. I have a much better and more fun suggestion. Room. Parties."

👽

Because the world of science fiction, fantasy, and horror is small when compared to the fan base of mystery and romance, the effectiveness of traditional forms of advertising can be negligible. Print advertising is mostly a waste of money and quite expensive. Because of the thin margins built into book publishing, web ads through Google aren't a smart option as the money you're paying per click through might surpass your net profit amount. Social media is free and can make a minor impact, but with tens of thousands of self-publishers pounding the social pavement, it is difficult to be heard above all the carnival barking. Corporate blogs are good at getting your message out to those already aware of your business, but unless you hit the jackpot and write a truly viral post, you're not likely to gain many new customers.

What is a cash-strapped small press to do?

Oddly, in a world of instant connectivity where half the drivers on any highway have their noses pressed against their smartphone screen, one of the most effective means of advertising is the personal touch. This is why small presses and self-publishers thrive on the convention circuit and vendor halls. We sit in stuffy, crowded ballrooms hoping for an opportunity to discuss our books with you. If you're interested, great, we'll sell you a book. If not, hopefully you'll remember us when you're looking for your next read. At most conventions, Apex doesn't make enough to cover food, gas, and lodging for the weekend. I consider food, gas, and lodging as advertising expenses and the cost of a great social networking opportunity. You have to view them as part of a long term advertising goal.

One way to get in touch with the most people in a short amount of time is to host a room party. It is a cost-effective way to connect with readers, other writers, other editors, and other publishers. The host will place flyers all over the venue (typically a hotel) advertising the event. You offer people snacks and free booze. In return, hundreds of attendees will filter in and out of your party throughout the evening. For a brief moment, they are captives to your ulterior motives.

One of my favorite conventions on my annual bookselling tour was Context. We always sold a ton of books. Also, Context was the first convention to invite me to be a guest of honor. Context is no more, but the memory of many good times remains.

Because Context was an "Apex Stronghold" (Another Maurice phrase), we decided that it would be the perfect place to begin the process of legend building. We would hold the very first Apex room party.

This party had to be memorable. Revelers would show up, have a blast, remember it as the 'Apex Party', and go out into the world-at-large and tell friends and family about the experience. The Apex name would spread. The legend would grow.

Here is where I tell you that I had never thrown a room party. I had never been thought of as someone who looked to party. Obviously, I needed help from an expert. I turned to the one man I knew who had the vision and experience to organize a memorable night of drunken revelry. That man was Geoffrey Girard.

Geoffrey Girard needs no legend building. The facts of his life are legend.

Angry after reading one of the annual Writers of the Future contest anthologies, Geoff felt like *he* should be a WotF winner. He pounded out a story in a couple of hours that he immediately mailed to the next contest. Of course, he won. Of course, it was also his first short story sale. His first novel (about cloned famous serial killers throughout history) sold for an unspeakably large advance and received a dual YA/adult thriller release (the first of its kind in the New York publishing business that anybody knows about). And I couldn't speak about the legend of the man without mentioning his hair. Geoffrey Girard has legendary hair—gorgeous brown locks that flow even in the lightest of breezes. He grows it out when he goes on tour with his rock band.

When Geoffrey Girard sets his mind to do something, he does it big.

God help us, Apex went "Full Girard" that weekend.

We reserved a suite that had two large rooms: a living room and a bedroom. The large living room would function as our dance floor. Girard built a DJ station out of the room's desk, strung up Christmas lights, and cleared off an area for dancing. The bedroom would work as the location for our bar and snacks. Trying to keep expenses to a minimum, I bought several cases of Natty Light, made up two jugs of hooch (blue and red) that we served out of clear plastic jugs, and an assortment of hard liquors for the occasional shot. I set up a folding card table to function as my bar. We switched off the main lights and hooked up several low watt lamps to create an ambient atmosphere in both rooms.

We were ready to rock and roll.

Crashing on the couch in the living room to catch my breath, I watched as Geoff lined guest chairs along the wall.

"Are you looking forward to dancing with your fans tonight?"

Dancing? I had performed some terrible body contortions out of sync to the music at my senior prom. But had I danced? No.

"Geoff, I'm not dancing," I explained. "Nobody is going to dance. We're geeks. Everybody will be lined up against the wall talking about Doctor Who and hating on Battlestar Galactica."

"I'll have you dancing before the night is over."

"You should set yourself some realistic goals," I said.

Girard winked. "I don't set goals. I accomplish goals."

Shaking my head, I decided to finish setting up for the party. Next to the bar, I placed a table of Apex swag. Three retractable Apex banners hung around the rooms. I even had special Apex alien head shot glasses on hand for the fans who wanted to do a shot with the infamous Apex publisher, of which I was certain there would be none.

We were ready and I even had time to grab a bite of dinner, if snacking on our spread of meats and cheeses counts as a meal. With a slice of cheddar midway to my mouth, I noticed Girard was monkeying around with a projector.

I popped the cheese in my mouth, swallowed, and asked, "What's that for?"

"You'll see. It's going to be cool."

The cheese felt like a lead ball rolling down my gullet. I had my doubts.

We opened our doors at 9 p.m., right on schedule.

The first song played was Britney Spears's "...Baby One More Time."

Britney! I rushed over and accosted Geoff. "What the hell is wrong with you?" I yelled over the din of bubblegum pop.

He shrugged and pointed at the projector. I followed the beam of projector light from its source to the ceiling where images flashed by in randomly timed intervals.

Zombies invading a shopping mall.

Flash

Eddie Vedder crowd-surfing.

Flash

HAL 9000's glowing red eye.

Flash

"What in the...?" somebody said.

I turned. Several people were transfixed; heads tilted upward, mouths gapped-open like the ends of exhaust pipes.

I waved my hands in front of Girard's face. He did a little shimmy and grooved to Britney Spears.

"Geoff!" I yelled.

He finally acknowledged me. "Awesome, right?" he asked, rhetorically.

"What is this?" I motioned to the slide show. The Black Dahlia with her horrible Glasgow smile appeared above us.

Geoff flipped his sexy brown locks out of his face. "It's the atmosphere. It's the element nobody will forget. Years from now, everyone that comes to this party, *your* Apex party, will tell their friends about the show."

I had no response.

"You're welcome." Geoff grabbed my shoulder and squeezed. Britney's vocals were replaced by Nine Inch Nail's "Closer".

A chicken having its head chopped off.

Flash

The cover of *Dark Faith*.

Flash

A preacher handling a rattlesnake in front of a crying congregation.

Flash

👽

The party started to peak around 11:30 p.m. Both rooms were packed, nearly shoulder to shoulder, with revelers. I tried a head count and lost track around 80. The place was sweltering, but nobody seemed to mind. To my surprise, geeks danced to Girard's odd mix of tunes like a congeries of palm trees blowing around in a hurricane. Others absently watched the slide show. A huge crowd surrounded the bar as I doled out free drinks.

The 'Shots with a Publisher' option was popular. Too popular. I started out strong. After I slammed back my eighth hit of vodka, I realized I would be face down and blacked out before midnight if I didn't pace myself. I cut back to half-shots, then quarter-shots. Between the booze and the socializing, I was riding high on Apex love and drinking in every moment of it.[15]

At one point, the music screeched to a halt and half the party cleared out. A security guard had been dispatched due to a noise complaint. I drunkenly explained that we were having a party, and that he was invited to dance with us, and that we were going to be quiet as mice.

Later that night, somebody pointed out two couples engaging in heavy petting on the bed. Ham flashbacks made my

---

[15] Meeting Jason was like a series of déjà vu moments, a loop of me browsing the Apex table, fingers trailing down spines before selecting the perfect one to make mine. It may have gone on forever if Jason hadn't spoken up one day.

"You look familiar. Have we met before?" He handed me my change.

I blushed and mumbled something about buying other Apex books in the past. Being the extreme introvert that I am, I kept my eyes firmly locked on the table of books before me, avoiding looking Jason as he tried to engage me in conversation. *Yay, he's talking to me! Oh damn, he's going to expect me to respond!* When he mentioned the Apex party later that night, I said I'd be there and scurried away.

A party! Someone invited me to a party! I would go! I would be social! I would look somewhere other than my shoes!

A ball of anxiety settled painfully in my stomach.

I went to the Apex party that night. I got to meet the rest of the Apex crowd, Jason was friendly, a cup of pink stuff that never seemed to lower no matter how much I drank was handed to me. I'm not sure what was in that pink stuff—even after all these years Jason won't tell me—but I think it may have included something that would leave me highly suggestible. *Work for Apex. Work for Apex. Work for Apex.* I held out as long as I could, but only a few months later I suddenly found that I was working for Apex. **(Lesley Conner, *Apex Magazine* managing editor)**

stomach clench, and I shooed both parties away to fornicate in their own beds.

Inexplicably, Maurice Broaddus's two young boys appeared. Or perhaps they share Maurice's innate ability to find any party within a certain mile range (Many consider this to be Maurice's superpower.) His boys were leaned back on the couch enjoying the image slide.

Topless New York City protestors.

Flash

A screen grab of a Liu Kang's "Dragon" fatality kill from Mortal Kombat 2.

Flash

Copulating walruses.

Flash

After I had ushered the underage invaders back to the Broaddus' hotel room, Maurice jumped up and took the dance floor. As a rhythm-impaired redneck, I harbor a deep jealousy for Mr. Broaddus's impressive array of moves. His dancing invigorated the crowd, and soon he had a group of geeky men and women busting it in a large circle.

Girard sidled up to me as I watched. "Go get in on some of that. Nobody cares if you suck."

"I'm a publisher," I sniffed. "I have a modicum of respect to maintain."

Girard stared at me. "You have a choice to make. Do you want to be remembered as the square that is boring, or do you want to be remembered as the square that knows how to have fun?"

He returned to his DJ stand, leaving me to muse over his question.

The quandary might have left me frozen in that spot, useless, boring, and helpless, had Nayad Monroe not appeared.

Nayad is a talented writer and editor and a longtime friend of mine. That night, when she walked in and brought the party to a momentary halt with her appearance, was the first time I ever laid eyes on her. She wore a glittery blue wig, a flowing, sparkling silver dress, and a luminescent smile. The woman was party goddess incarnate. The dancing circle opened to accept their new queen, and Nayad pushed Maurice aside as the nucleus of attention. Dozens of new dancers flocked to her, answering her calls to dance.

I was hypnotized by the movement, by the music. Unconsciously, my left foot started to tap in time with the song. The dance floor called to me.

"Nice party."

I watched Nayad gyrate. Perhaps, just perhaps, I could mimic some of her moves and not make an idiot of myself.

"Hey, nice party!"

I blinked. Somebody was speaking to me. Somebody I didn't recognize.

A young lady stood nearby. She nursed a fancy beer. I reckoned her age to be mid-20s. She had striking raven-black wavy hair, dark red lips, and unblemished pale white skin that contrasted nicely with a well-fitted concert tee.

I blushed. Here I was sweating like a struggling pack mule in the Mojave. My Apex T-shirt stuck to my belly and displayed a patchwork of sweaty dampness.

"Hi," I mumbled.

"What?" she said, louder. She drew closer, leaning in with her ear. The young lady smelled like an intoxicated mix of cherry lip balm, cigarettes, and beer.

I felt like a terrified middle school kid. Even with liberal doses of alcohol bravado, my usual dashing charm and wit betrayed me. "I have to work the bar," I mumbled, and walked away.

She followed. Persistent, she was. At least now I had a table of alcohol between the two of us.

"I'm Elaine Blose." She held out her hand.

Dammit, my hand was sweaty. I gripped hers with mine and introduced myself. To her credit, she didn't flinch when making contact with my clammy skin.

She eyed the sign hanging next to the bar stating "Free: Shots with the Publisher."

"Will you do a shot with me?"

I gulped, nervous but it seemed safe enough. "Pick your poison," I said. She chose bourbon. This Kentucky boy was impressed. I poured us quarter-shots and reached to pick mine up.

Elaine stayed my hand. "I don't think so. The sign says a *shot* with the publisher. That's a sip, not a shot. What kind of Kentucky boy can't hold his bourbon?"

Well, the challenge had been made. "Okay, okay." I filled our glasses to the very top. We said 'Cheers' and tossed them back.

I tried to hide my watering eyes. Elaine smiled, as though she had taken a drink of chilled water.

"Would you like to dance?" she asked.

"I don't dance."

"Come on! Everybody at this party can tell you're a huge square. Dance with me, and you're not such a loser. Don't dance with me, and it's squaresville for you, mister."

I eyed her suspiciously. Her pitch sounded suspiciously familiar. "Did Geoff Girard send you over here?"

"Who's that?"

"Right."

She grabbed my clammy hand and led me out from behind the table of booze. Closer and closer we inched to the dancing mob.

"I got no moves," I objected. "They're all gonna laugh at me."

"Just do what I do."

She danced and did it well. I kind of moved side to side. There was no rhythm or effort. Everybody was staring at me. I felt it in my gut. Never had I been so embarrassed.

But, as the night wore on, I started trying harder. The bourbon sloshing in my stomach eventually found my bloodstream and I suddenly cared little for what everybody else might think. I joined the crowd of dance-a-holics. Girard came over and bumped hips with me. He smiled like a possum who had just found a sack of spoiled burgers in a garbage can.

"Told you," he said.

"Well played, Mr. Girard, sending Elaine Blose over. She's incredibly persuasive"

"Who's that?"

I shooed him away and shook my moneymaker.

Elaine laughed at me. "Okay, I'm definitely buying an Apex book tomorrow."

I pumped my fist. The first sale I'd ever made thanks to my inability to dance!

The party slowly wound down. By 2 a.m., only six of us remained. We sat and stared skyward at the ceiling.

A roomful of kittens.

Flash

The galley slave ship from *Ben-Hur*.

Flash

The fish baby cover to *Apex Digest* issue 5.

Flash

Maurice, one of the people determined to close the party down, looked over at Girard. "How did you decide which pictures to use in the slide show?"

Geoff took a sip of beer. Stared up at fish baby. "They're all things I suspect Sizemore dreams about."

Later that day, dozens of people took the time to tell me about how much fun they had had at the Apex party. Most asked me if we were doing it again next year.

"It depends," I would say. "If we have a good sales weekend in the vendor hall we'll definitely be back."

We set a record for sales at that Context.

Legendary, even.

Building the Legend of Apex
Eyewitness Rebuttal

Elaine Blose

I love to travel. For years I was always jetting off some-where overseas to explore the world and connect with friends. One such time I attended WorldCon in Glasgow, Scotland with my friend Paul from Sweden.

Then it happened.

The year was escaping from me and I had no travel plans and needed a week away from work. Cruising the internet I found a small convention called Context in Columbus. I'd been to a few WorldCons but not a small convention such as this. Also, I had friends who had moved to Columbus for better jobs who were begging me to visit.

While Ohio's state capital city isn't Australia or France, nor is it exotic or foreign, it was still away from home.

I made arrangements to visit my friends and registered for Context. I'll be honest, I wasn't expecting much. No one was attending the con with me. While I have friends who like sci-fi, they were not big enough nerds to attend a convention with me.

I had a vague idea of what to expect at the con. I knew there would be panels, there would be like-minded people, and best of all, there would be parties. I was looking forward to it, even though I would be on my own at the con.

I arrived in Columbus on Thursday morning and stayed with my friends. Friday I went to the hotel and checked in, then went to registration to get my badge. I was surprised at how friendly everyone was, and that so many people introduced themselves to me in the registration line.

One I remember was Jason Sizemore. I could tell he was a bit bashful, but hey, a lot of writers and nerds are, so I thought nothing of it.

I saw him again that evening at a small room party. I remember sitting in a chair next to him and not giving it much thought. He seemed like a nice guy but he was very quiet and didn't speak much.

Basically, I had no idea at this point that he was the owner of Apex, I had no idea of what the real Jason Sizemore was like, and in short, I didn't talk to him because of any of these things. I hadn't gone to the con to network with editors or anything of the sort, because I still knew at this point that everything I attempted to write sucked. Plain and simple. So there was no point in me trying to schmooze my way to publication.

That night, Jason did mention that he was having a party on Saturday night. He sat there and told me, "I'm having a party tomorrow. You should come. It will be better than this one."

I thought, "Yeah, right. I'm sure it will be just like this one, just a bunch of people standing around talking about all aspects of speculative fiction and related matter." Nothing wild, nothing memorable.

"Sure, I'll come. Will there be free beer?"

"Yep, in fact we will have a well-stocked bar." Then he added, "My party is going to be the party of the century. People will talk about it for years to come. It is going to legendary." This was said by Mr. Bashful.

I didn't give it another thought until the next night.

I had another great day on Saturday meeting new people and making all kinds of friends. In all, I was having a blast. All day, I noticed flyers everywhere for the Apex party.

That night a couple people and I were milling about when we started hearing rumors about this kickass party in progress. Having no more panels to go to that night. I navigated my way through the hotel to the designated room.

Before I got to the room the sound of music and laughter drifted down the hall. The room's darkness was illuminated with Christmas lights and bizarre images projected on the ceiling. Techno music blared as a few souls danced in the center of one of the rooms.

It was difficult to carry on a conversation, but no one seemed to mind. I saw a man with brown, flowing locks near the source of the images and tending the bar.

Off along the wall, I saw Jason standing there like a stereotypical wallflower. I began to approach him and then I saw a sign that said "Free: Shots with the Publisher".

I figured if there was a cure for being a wallflower it was booze. So I came up to him and said, "So, are you going to do a shot with me?"

"Ah, sure," he said, not looking very confident. "Pick your poison." He pointed to the selection of liquor. I chose bourbon and he poured the glass only a quarter full.

I looked at the glass he tried to hand me and said, "I thought we were doing shots, not little sips."

Sweat broke out on his forehead as he topped off the shots. We said cheers and tossed them back. His face made a grimace I couldn't understand since I was quite certain the booze had been watered down.

"So what do you think?" he asked me.

"Nice party, I like it. You even got Britney Spears playing."

"This isn't Britney."

"Yeah, it is, this is her new song 'Gimme More.' Please don't ask how I know this."

Finally he gave a small laugh. "I'll have to talk to my DJ about this." He pointed to the man with brown hair that should have been on a shampoo commercial.

"I like the images." I pointed to the ceiling. "It's a nice touch."

"Oh, well thank you, that was my idea," he said beaming.

"You ready to cut the rug then?"

"What? No, we can't ruin the carpet or the hotel will charge me an arm and a leg. Already had security here tonight."

"What? Security has been here already? Sweet!" You could tell he puffed out his chest just a little. "But what I meant was, are you ready to dance?"

His chest puff deflated in an instant. "Oh, no, I mean, well, I can't dance."

"Sure you can. Just look at what everybody else is doing. Kind of go with it and just remember everyone is probably drunk so they won't remember to judge you tomorrow." I grabbed his hand and pulled him out amongst the other dancers having a great time.

He was right. The man couldn't dance.[16] However, he put forth a noble effort and after a short time I could tell he loosened up and got somewhat comfortable.

The night wore on, and like all good things it came to an end. The next day, being severely sleep-deprived and exhausted beyond belief and yet strangely content and very happy, I wondered my way down to the dealer's room.

There I found Jason selling books. I bought quite a few for myself and we talked about writing. He urged me to send him something, but now it was my turn to be bashful and I told him I would, but he would probably think it sucked.

When I returned to my friend's house to spend Sunday night instead of driving home, I think they wondered what exactly had gone on over the weekend.

I have learned over the years since then that some cons stick out in your mind more than others. Despite all the others I have attended since that one, the party is the one thing about it that I don't think I will ever forget. The whole weekend was awesome, but that party really was the butter-cream frosting on top.

I kept going back to Context faithfully every year since until its untimely demise. And every year, somebody made

---

[16] I believe the shots Elaine had with me are clouding her recall regarding my dancing. **(Jason Sizemore)**

mention of that particular party. There have been Apex parties since, but none has ever topped that first one.

Why?

Very simple. That party was the stuff of legends.

Building the Legend of Apex
Eyewitness Rebuttal

Geoffrey Girard

I 've been asked to write a rebuttal of some kind. But, what to deny?

It *was* a great party. Jason *did* dance his ass off. And, I *do* have great hair.

Besides, saying anything else could expose a lie/operation which goes back almost a decade.

So instead I started a draft exploring the merits and consequence of community, the complexities of public identity, the wrangling of introverts, and the undisputable contributions of Britney Spears. Lost steam around page sixteen, when I was still defining *community*.

I've deleted all that, and now this: the truth.

I met Jason a decade ago at Hypericon, in Nashville. He had the very first issue of *Apex Science Fiction and Horror Digest* in his hands. I had a story in the latest *Writers of the Future*. Neither one of us knew what we were doing. It was arranged that we ended up on a panel together. No one showed up. Seriously, Jason and I were the only ones in the room. So, we just talked to each other for an hour. About publishing and writing and shit that scares us. We've been friends ever since. Can't tell you how happy the folks back home were.

When I was first dispatched here to Teegeeack, befriending Jason was paramount. Don't be so impressed with the "banged a story out in a few hours" for *Writers of the Future* baloney. The Galactic Confederacy had gotten me into that anthology with one phone call. It's all about who you know. (And as for the missing attendees, asking then-up-and-coming author Matt Wallace to stand outside the conference room door and tell people to fuck off was like asking gravity to work.)

An hour alone with Jason was more than enough time. He was hypnotized four times. One of those times leads to this....

The party.

Party expectations for geek writers (and editors) are typically month-long whimsical predictions of gunshots and fire-trucks and hookers and cocaine-laced pretzels and playing Twister with Neil Gaiman and naked unicorns. Like *Caligula*. Or *Monkeybone*, maybe. But 99% of the time, right around 10:30, reality sets in: *regular* pretzels, and lots of guys in black t-shirts asking "So, um, what are you working on?"

It was important, however, that Jason get his fantasy. Thus that 1%.

For example:

There was no slideshow. No pictures of snake charmers or fish babies or Liu Kang or anything else. The projector showed only one image:

An image first implanted into a young Kentuckian in June 1974.

The "slideshow" Jason watched that night — thanks to the Nashville-set trigger of the word "baby" fifteen times in twenty seconds — was NOT things I "thought he dreamed of." They were, quite literally, things HE dreamed of. Everyone else was staring only at the alien head. Maurice's kids weren't gaping in amazement at "naked people on the ceiling." They were just trying to figure out what the hell Jason was so fascinated with.

Everyone was in on it. Maurice acted like he was seeing the same pictures Jason did. Author/editor Jerry Gordon pretended he didn't really know anyone and just *happened* to be making lifelong friends in a single evening. Nayad's astral projection was one of her best ever; actually had Jason convinced she'd come from TEXAS(!) for CONTEXT???! The Soylent Green looked and tasted exactly like cheese. Wrath James White dropped by in an Elaine Blose costume.

The security guard was not asked to dance after the "music screeched to a halt." He screeched when we killed him. Then, when there was that awkward moment at the door when Jason walked over to see what was going on when we were dragging his corpse from the room. One *Weekend at Bernie's* scene later, we were down the hall and out the back of the hotel. Later that night, two of the party attendees helped me get rid of the body. They seemed pretty into it and have kept their mouths shut so far and I'm not gonna say anything more other that in my defense, their father should have thought about what was going on that weekend before bringing them to the con.

Post-security, it got kinda crazy. Gary A. Braunbeck showed up with Erma Bombeck and Dave Brubeck. Lucy Snyder arrived with John Schneider and Zack Snyder and Rob Schneider and Roy Scheider. Into the room came Angus Scrimm, Abdul Alhazred, Jessica 6, Tetsuo, Carter Burke, the ghost of Lizzie Borden, Walter Skinner, Charles Ingalls, Lucy Pevensie, Joey Wheeler, Ray Harryhausen, Mike Damone, the head from *Re-Animator*, Charles Beaumont, The Great Gazoo, Tinky Winky, Witchiepoo, Ada Wong, "Mutt" Lange, Chazz Michael Michaels, Edie Sedgwick, The Thompson Twins, Maxwell Edison, Queen Elizabeth II, the goldbug from the Richard Scarry books, Daryl Dixon, Harper Lee, Nosferatu, Wilson Fisk, The Babadook, Martha Stewart, Jeffrey Jacobson, Willow Rosenberg, Pete Best, Pete Rose, The Lindbergh baby, Jaina Proudmoore, Annabelle, Hal Incandenza, Medusa, Beowulf, a Zuni fetish doll named "He Who Kills," Charles Dexter Ward, Nikola Tesla, Jodie Foster, Mrs. Lovett, Candyman, Jane Goodall, The Cool Ghoul, Cujo, Gale King, Stephen King, Don King, Billie Jean King, Lady Chatterley, Clara Barton, Dracula's Daughter, Mechagodzilla, Jennifer Tilly, Sadako Yamamura, Ryan Seacrest, Noah, Captain Howdy, Pillow Pants, Rumer Willis, that albino guy from *Foul Play*, Paul Williams, Joan Jett, David Foster Wallace, Jubal Harshaw, Pennywise, the Toxic Avenger, two mannequins from *Tourist Trap*, Annie Wilkes, Ashton Youboty, the Queef Sisters, Kevin Bacon and others.

Finally, emissaries from the Galactic Confederacy appeared. People took turns meeting them in the back room, and the noun and verb of "probe" were augmented for everyone. This is also when Jason began, unknowingly, serving Pan Galactic Gargle Blasters. Shots with the editor. Ha! Also, Fester-Bester Tester brought a huge duffle bag of drugs: Krrf, Drencrom, Kerbango, Betaphenethylamine, Hazia, Trellium-D, Bug Powder, Black Lotus, and enough melange to give half of Columbus blue eyes.

People *did* dance. Half the room crafted a drinking game out of solving the Lament Configuration and the cenobites got so fucking wasted. A couple people did the Kessel Run in *eleven* parsecs. A few of us invented the musical note "H" and wrote half a dozen killer songs. Everyone made love. Someone danced faster than light. Two walruses copulated on the bed and Jason chased them out of the room. Later, Tars Tarkas convinced him it was just a picture on the slideshow. Yes, Neil Gaiman played Twister. Eventually, we all sat in a big circle and everyone shouted out random words while Gary A. Braunbeck wrote the Great American Novel from our cries. It was 150k words. It was a horror novel. And it was really, really good. Then he deleted it. Everyone laughed and then rolled around the ceiling together for a while.

The party lasted six days.

Throughout it all, the alien emissaries kept close giant black eyes on the guest of honor. Making notes. Grinning like proud parents. Jason was living up to their expectations and plans. But they agreed he still had much to accomplish here on Teegeeack as an editor, writer, friend, and dancer. They agreed they could wait a little longer yet, and that the wait was worth it.

After, Jason slept like a rock. Thing 1 and Thing 2 helped me clean up. The aliens gave me more hair in thanks for all I'd done. And then they gave me the trigger for when Jason would finally be called beyond to fulfill his ultimate destiny. (Hint: "Baby, can't you see, I'm calling a guy like you….")

To be continued….

A 2011 AP-GfK poll revealed that 77 percent of adults believe angels are real. We're talking the floating down from heaven, halo glowing around the head, majestic wings variety. Angels watch over God's flock of troublesome lambs and guard us from harm. Scripture tells us in Psalms chapter 91, verse 11 (King James Version) "For he shall give his angels charge over thee, to keep thee in all thy ways."

Count me in that 77 percent of adults who believe.

Depictions of angels through time have changed little. If the great artistic minds of past and current humankind are to be believed, these workhorses of heaven dress as though they belong to a cult: flowing white robes, beatific smiles, chubby naked children clowning about, an urge to intrude upon your life.

I've seen angels. Two of them, though they looked slightly different than our culture's popular artistic renditions. My angels were beautiful, with ample décolletage, magical glitter, and gorgeous flowing skirts.

Without my two guardian angels... well, I shudder to think of how my trip to Archon in St. Louis would have turned out.

To meet Sara M. Harvey is to be in the presence of a Force of Nature. She's a charming, erudite, Southern lady with a delightful twist of SoCal snark. Her boundless energy and winning smile is nature's anti-depressant.

As you can see, I think highly of her.

I had been running Apex for three or four years. The company was doing well on the coasts and north of my home base of Kentucky. Sales from the Midwest were miniscule, so I set my sights toward the Mississippi River and decided to travel and meet the fandom in the Heartland. I wanted their money.

Sara had suggested I bring the Apex show to Archon, a fairly large media and fan event held each year in St. Louis. She and Elizabeth Donald—a fellow vendor and author—described the crowd as being book-friendly. It was within driving distance, Sara would be in attendance, and Jacqueline Carey (I get the fanboy quivers typing her name!) was scheduled to be a guest. A weekend with Sara, meeting Jacqueline Carey (quiver), and making money. This promised to be a magnificent weekend!

As so often with my plans, the heart was willing, but the body was not.

Archon, as it turns out, is a rather fancy convention. The venue that year was in a clean hotel—I'd say moderately upscale, even. The vendor hall was large and roomy. I had a good feeling about the weekend. Even the slow Friday evening sales didn't deter my optimism. Most Friday evenings in vendor halls are lackluster in terms of volume and interest. Folks drive a long way for conventions and prefer to meet up with old friends and attend panels headlined by famous people rather than go shopping.

Sara was popular at Archon. The event organizers had filled her schedule with panels and demos (besides being a talented writer, Sara's also a highly skilled costumer and teaches the craft in her spare time), so I saw little of her on Friday. Once the vendor hall closed, I ventured out to engage in afterhours activities. Archon had sectioned off a large hallway where attendees of legal age could get free beer. Even though I don't drink beer—frou-frou drinks all the way for me—I was impressed by the offering. Lots of people had their rooms open for socializing and room parties. I had found my Mecca. I had found my *people*.

Except I wasn't feeling well. All day my stomach had been giving me problems. I also felt unusually fatigued. The foreboding sense that I might be coming down with an intestinal ailment or even the flu hovered over me like a storm cloud. I could not let that happen. I would not let that happen. The weekend beckoned me. I had Jacqueline Carey to meet!

In a rare display of prudence, I elected to skip all alcohol, limit my socializing, save my strength, and go back to my room to rest and sleep.

This self-imposed confinement wasn't so bad. I had been placed in a nice suite with a large screen television, a couch, and other fineries.

I told myself that taking it easy the night before would give me the reserves of strength to push through the weekend. I had money to make. Friends to greet. It takes a lot of energy to keep up with Sara Harvey. But despite turning in early, the next morning, I felt no better. In fact, my stomach gurgled and complained much worse than it had the day before.

After a light breakfast of fruit and granola, I made my way to the Apex table. Sara was already there, bright, bouncy, and happy.

"Good morning, boss!"

She calls me 'boss'. I never stop getting a kick out of it.

"Oh, you look more pale than usual," she said, concerned.

My stomach agitation had grown to an uncomfortable level. A gnawing pain invaded my side.

"I don't feel well," I said.

Like most people when they hear somebody state this, Sara took a step back. "Are you contagious?"

I put my hand against my left side. "Sadly, I don't think so."

"You go back to your room and relax. I'll watch the table until 11." She had a panel at 11 and five more hours of Archon events to do that day.

I nodded. I needed to be fit for the long section of the day when I wouldn't have table backup. "Okay, I'll be back soon."

The walk back to my room was lengthy, so I made haste. As I exited the vendor hall, I ran into an old friend.

I have the worst luck.

"Hello, Mr. Sizemore, I need to speak with you for a minute." Hickory Adams, dammit. My gaze was immediately drawn to his coarse eyebrows, which had grown since I'd last seen him. They stuck out beyond his face like two white bundles of wires.

"Mr. Adams," I said, "I don't mean to be rude, but I'm really in a hurry."

The old fella squinted at me. "Funny, because that seems to be the case every time we talk. If one isn't a young and pretty thing, then you're too busy to talk."

A sharp pain stabbed my left side. My stomach gurgled in dismay.

"That is categorically untrue, Mr. Adams," I said. "I'm not feeling well and I need to get back to my room."

"Who's the comely lady working your table this weekend? Is it another sixteen-year-old? Or let me guess, another college intern coed looking for extra credit on her resume?"

"Sara Harvey. She's one of my authors." As I said it, I knew I was only making matters worse.

"I know Ms. Harvey very well. Just your type, right? I heard her call you 'boss'. Some little inappropriate publisher/author game you play?"

"Look, I need to go."

"Can't you give my latest novel pitch a fair shake?"

I bit my lip, holding back the building pain, the scream.

"I've set this one on a generational ship. The earth is being destroyed by a liberal agenda to monetize tree leaves."

"Damn liberals always destroying the planet," I managed to say.

"After twenty years, the heroes on the G-ship discover that all the women are barren."

I frowned. "That's awful."

"I agree, Mr. Sizemore, that is a terrible predicament for humankind."

My stomach cramped. "No, the novel idea. It's terrible."

"It's 455,000 words. We can split it into three different books. A series."

"Oh God, I think I'm going to puke." Stomach acid burned my throat. My left side was one persistent nexus of pain and agony.

A mesh of purple veins spread over Hickory's face as he mounted his opprobrium. "Mr. Sizemore, you are the biggest asshole in the business. I'm filing a formal complaint with the SFWA."

That was the last thing I heard him say. The pain had become unbearable and I'd broken out in a sweat. I had to get to my room before I lost my breakfast and left my mark in the hotel hallways.

By this point, I was 100% certain I was in the grips of a kidney stone attack.

I've been plagued by kidney stones since I was 22. Over the past decade, I had battled three major stones that required lithotripsy surgery, where the urologist uses lasers to blast the stones into smaller pieces. Sometimes the stone will pass without further incident. Other times, you can flush your system with water and draw the stone out. I had been through this song and dance before and knew the steps.

Being a frequent kidney stone sufferer, I always come prepared and pack some Vicodin on every trip. If I have stone problems, I pop the Vicodin, wait on them to take the edge off the pain, and seek medical assistance if I can't flush the stones out after eight hours. At least, that's the game plan.

Back in the room, the first thing I did was vacate the contents of my stomach—not that I had a choice in the matter. I knew I had to get the pain medicine in me quickly before dry heaves set in and I wouldn't be able to keep the pills down.

I crawled to my suitcase and rummaged through all the pockets to discover I had left my Vicodin at home.

Uh oh.

The only thing I had was a bottle of ibuprofen. I took the maximum suggested dose of 800mg and drank a glass of water.

Anybody reading this who has suffered through kidney stones knows the effectiveness of 800mg of ibuprofen against the pain. The muscles along the urethral wall cramp and spasm as they try to push the offending obstruction out of the urethra. Imagine the worst muscle cramp you've ever endured. Now place the epicenter of that cramp in a spot just below your kidney on your lower back. That pain is a tsunami and 800mg of ibuprofen is a small boat in the way.

The nausea was growing. Without my Vicodin, I had to find medical attention. The pain left me shaky and not thinking straight. All I knew was that I needed an emergency room. I looked through the phonebook for hospitals. This was before I had a smartphone and Google Maps. The yellow pages listed some hospitals, but I had no clue how close they were or how to get to them.

I grabbed the keys to my truck and stumbled to the hotel lobby where I found the concierge. The concierge was a young guy, probably no more than twenty years old. I explained to him that I was having kidney stone pain and needed to know where I could find the nearest emergency room. He wrote down some sketchy directions, and wished me luck.

Thinking back, I don't know why the guy didn't offer to call me a cab. Or possibly have the hotel escort me to the nearest clinic. Perhaps I should have thought of it myself, but my brain had a singular focus: keeping me from falling to the floor and curling into the fetal position.

I made it to my truck and started to follow the directions I was given. Twice I had to pull over to throw up. Twice more I had to stop to scream and squirm my way through the pain.

After about fifteen minutes, I realized I was lost. And not just lost; I was lost in what looked to be a sketchy part of St. Louis. Half the buildings were run down, the other half were tore down. Not many people were about. Eventually, I spotted a group of teenagers loitering about on the steps of a burnt out house. The pain was so bad that it made me forget that I'm scared of young people. I pulled over and rolled down my passenger side window.

"I need help," I gasped out. My voice had grown husky due to the multiple regurgitations of stomach contents.

The teenagers, four of them in all, looked at each other, puzzled by my appearance. One lanky kid had his head shaved, tattoos etched up and down his arms, and sported a skullcap and a mouthful of crooked teeth. He spoke up for the group.

"You're not from around here, are you?" he asked.

"No. Kentucky."

Laughter. "Thought so. You talking like you're straight on up out of *Deliverance*."

The kids laughed. I heard a couple of "Squeal for me, piggy" jokes.

"I need help. Can you show me to the hospital?"

Skullcap frowned at me. "Old man, you tripping on something?"

"I need Vicodin...."

More laughter. "Don't we all, Kentucky. You got any?"

"No. Sorry."

The lanky kid opened the door and took a seat in my truck. "Yo, you fools, I'm taking Kentucky to the hospital. Be back in a few."

I pulled out into the street and slumped over the steering wheel, setting off the truck's horn.

"You okay to drive, brother?"

"No," I said. He gave me directions and I followed.

The hospital was only a few blocks away. I got out of the truck, and for some reason I thought Skullcap would go inside with me. As he turned to leave, I called out to him.

"Thank you."

"Remember, anybody asks, you don't know me, right?"

I blinked. "Right."

"Good on you, Kentucky boy. Good on you," he said. And then he was gone.

The hospital's parking lot was empty except for three vehicles.

None of them were ambulances. Even through unimaginable pain, I found this odd. The emergency room door slid open, so I entered. What other choice did I have?

Inside sat a skinny black lady behind a desk protected by bulletproof glass. She acted surprised to see me.

The waiting room consisted of a pair of dented, tan fold out aluminum chairs. Half the lights were off. One even flickered. I began to wonder if I'd walked into a first person shooter video-game: perhaps *Dead Space* or *F.E.A.R. 2*.

A pain wrenched my side and I doubled over. I dry heaved right there in the middle of the empty room. The lady behind the desk stood up, concerned.

"Honey, what's wrong?" she asked.

Through clenched teeth and heavy breaths, I said "Kidney stones."

Another lady appeared—this one wearing a nurse's uniform. She took me by the elbow and led me through a door where a gurney rested against the hallway wall. "Lay down here." As I gasped and cried in pain, she took my vitals.

"Did you know your blood pressure is elevated?"

I was so desperate for medical assistance that I bit back a snarky response. "No."

"The doctor will be out to see you in a minute."

I may have passed out. I don't recall. My next memory was sticking my bare ass in the air to receive a shot of morphine. The agony receded. The world came into momentary focus.

I looked around. I was still on the gurney in the hallway. The doorways up and down the hallway were covered with opaque plastic hanging above the frame. Where were the doors? Why was this place so deserted? Had I fallen into the *Silent Hill* universe?

A young doctor, maybe twenty-seven years old, patted me on the shoulder. "Feel better?"

I nodded. He'd given me morphine. This man was my hero.

"Tell me your symptoms."

I gave him a rundown, complete with medical history.

"Yes, it sounds like kidney stones. But I can't give you any more pain medicine without a proper diagnosis. Lucky for you, the x-ray machine here still works."

"Why is this place so empty?" I asked. I noticed my words were slurred—an effect of the morphine.

"That accent is awesome! You're not from around here, are you?"

I shook my head no.

"What's your name?"

"Jason Sizemore. I'm from Kentucky."

"Ah, okay. I was afraid you had suffered brain damage."

This guy had jokes.

"Anyway, this hospital is closed. The emergency room closes tonight at midnight. So whatever is wrong with you, we have to have you out of here before then. Lucky for you, I think I remember how to take x-rays. Who needs techs, right?"

I get the x-rays and, back in the hallway, doze off. The doctor woke me up with a gentle prod. "I see what appears to be a two-centimeter blockage in your left urethra. Your kidney appears undamaged and normal sized. I can give you another shot, a script for Vicodin, and you can be on your way."

Then he was gone. Even in a hospital devoid of patients, the doctor moved as though in a hurry.

The nurse returned and asked me a few questions. "Do you have anybody who can take you home or to another hospital?"

In fact, I did not. My wife was in Lexington with our baby. I was six hours from home and trapped in a scary hospital. I could call her. Theoretically, she could fly out the next day, and then drive me home in my truck. But there was no way she could get to me before midnight.

I mumbled. I must have been pitiful because the nurse put her hand on my cheek and said, "Poor thing."

She leaned closer. "Anybody? A friend? A guardian angel?"

Then I remembered. Sara Harvey. I was too doped to talk, so I fumbled in my pocket and drew out my crappy flip top phone. I found Sara's number and handed it to the nurse.

I had told the nurse that two beautiful angels would be coming to save me. She cooed, "Okay, okay, whatever you say Mr. Sizemore" and stroked my head.

The next couple of hours are hazy. I remember getting another morphine shot. Apparently it was the last bit of injectable pain medicine they had remaining. Lucky me! I slept in the hallway and had terrible dreams. At some unknown interval later, I awoke to the sound of the desk clerk arguing with a familiar voice.

Sara Harvey at Archon
(Photo credit Elizabeth Donald)

"He has red hair. Has an accent. He's wearing a T-shirt bearing a giant alien head."

"I'm sorry, ma'am, but I can't let you back there dressed like that."

"Oh, please. *Whatever.*"

A door opened. Two women appeared. *My* two angels. Glitter adorned their faces. They wore black leather corsets that lifted their bosoms to their collarbones. The fading afternoon light shone from behind them as the clerk stood with her arms crossed, holding the door open. The angels were beautiful. The doctor, the nurse, and the clerk stared at them, mouths agape .

Sara rush over to my side.

"Oh, honey, you're okay," she said, placing her hand on my cheek. "We're here to take you home."

Sara and her friend Katie Yates took me back to my hotel room. They had dressed up for the Saturday night masquerade parties. I felt bad that I was making them miss time with their friends, but grateful to be back at the convention venue, safe and sound. That night I took pain and anti-nausea medicine, drank a gallon of water, and slept. I tried to flush the stone out, but to no avail. The pain did not recede, so I had to keep taking Vicodin. That meant I couldn't drive myself home. Sara stopped by the room several times to check on me, making sure I took my medicine and that I was comfortable. She even stole my Mt. Dew and gave me a bracing lecture about the unhealthy benefits of sugared sodas.

That evening, Sara and my wife Susan discussed our options. Susan could fly out the next day and drive me home late Sunday night. The other option was that Sara would drive me home Sunday afternoon in my truck. Her husband, Matt, would follow in their car. From there they would depart together from Lexington back to Nashville. For reasons I don't remember, we chose the Harvey Taxi Service.

There are lots of other things I don't remember from that Sunday. Like most of the drive back from St. Louis to Lexington. Apparently, I was the most charming and entertaining I had ever been with Sara Harvey. Pain, delirium, and Vicodin can work powerful miracles!

Perhaps Sara, Matt, and Katie are not the mystical type of guardian angels the Good Book describes (though Sara would probably argue they are), but they made sure I made it home safe and that I didn't suffer more than I had to.

They're the best type of angels a guy can have: awesome friends.

Stoned and Delirious
Eyewitness Rebuttal

Sara M. Harvey

Archon in St. Louis is one of my most favorite conventions. They have a great turnout and treat the guests well. I have had many a delightful dinnertime conversations up in the Green Room with the likes of Darth Maul and Fry from *Futurama*. Probably the most memorable year was 2008, and NOT just because it was functioning as my and my husband's quasi-honeymoon. Oh, no, we barely even got around to any of that.

By now, the story of Sizemore's kidney stone attack at Archon is con-legend. And how I stole all his Mountain Dew[17] (I swear that man had a Costco-sized flat of it in his room) and replaced it with water, and how he woke to chicken soup and granola bars every four hours to take his meds with (seriously, the con's hospitality staff had his schedule down and called me if I wasn't there waiting for a fresh supply of grub for him!), and there may have been something about me and my friend Katie in corsets and glitter. And that stuff's all true!

But there's a lot people don't know. In fact, Sizemore doesn't even know, bless his heart, he was in too much pain and too doped up to notice, much less remember.

I knew on Saturday morning that he wasn't feeling well. I told him to go back to bed and I'd watch the booth until it was time for my panels. He promised to come and tag out before I had to leave.

But he didn't.

I called his cell phone and, at first, it simply rang and rang and rang into oblivion.

---

[17] Of all the crimes committed against me, this one ranks among the worst! You just don't steal a country boy's Mt. Dew. **(Jason Sizemore)**

I tried again and this time it connected, momentarily, before becoming overcome with static and disconnecting.

Third time was the charm, but it jumped straight to voicemail. I left a message saying that I was worried about him and to please call, meanwhile, I was going to leave my husband at the booth and go give my panels.

When I returned to the dealer's room, Matt was still at the Apex table, looking fretful.

"Sizemore hasn't been back?"

"Nope," he said.

"Ok, that's odd. Hang tight, let me see if I can reach him."

Again the cell phone went directly to voicemail. I called over to the hotel and had them ring his room, there was no answer there, either.

Now, I was really worried. But there was naught to do about it since he couldn't be reached.

The moment the dealer's room closed, I called again, but still no answer. I went to the hotel desk and asked if I could have someone open the door to his room, terribly afraid something awful had happened and he was incapacitated or worse.

The clerk heard me out and nodded, he lifted the phone for a manager, then slowly set it down.

"Wait...we had a gentleman come by and ask directions to the hospital. Said he was having kidney stones, that he gets them all the time, but he didn't have his meds with him this time."

"Oh, so he's not here, then?"

"I haven't seen him come back. But if he went to the ER, he's probably still in the waiting room."

We both had a laugh about that. I asked to go to his room to check anyway and found that it was, indeed, devoid of Sizemore. I left another message on his cell phone.

With nothing left to do but sit and worry, I decided to get dressed for the evening. Which at Archon meant corsets and glitter and fabulosity. A group of us girls were primping and preening in Katie's room when my phone rang.

The connection was terrible, but I could hear Sizemore's feeble voice on the other end.

"Boss? Is that you? Where are you? Are you okay?"

He made some noises at me, then someone else came on the line. I couldn't tell if the speaker was man or woman, the voice was so indistinct, sounding as if it was coming from very far away.

"You need to come get him," the speaker told me. "Now."

And then the line went dead.

I had no idea whatsoever where he might have gone. But Katie was a local and she went with me to interrogate the front desk clerk. She did not like what he had to say.

"You sent him where?!"

He cringed away from her fury. "It's the closest ER..."

Katie swore loudly enough to grab the attention of everyone in the lobby and then pulled me out to her car. "He's at the ghetto hospital, the one the county has been trying to condemn for years. I didn't think it was even still operational. I know they stopped admitting patients a while ago."

"But the ER is still open?"

"Apparently. You said he called you from there?"

"I guess...?"

True to the clerk's directions, the ER was just minutes away and true to Katie's fears, it not only looked abandoned but it was in a neighborhood that I'd definitely consider "sketchy." Sizemore's car was the only other one in the parking lot. It had to be his, with the Kentucky plates and Apex Publications bumper sticker.

We rushed inside and met a very confused-looking security guard.

"What are you doing here?"

"We need to pick up her friend," Katie told him.

"Ain't nobody here, the hospital is closed."

"He has to be," I insisted, "I just talked to him on the phone, he came into the ER. The hotel sent him here."

The security guy actually laughed at that. "You'd better have words with that hotel, lady. This hospital is closed."

He allowed us to step past him into the ER's waiting room. Most of the lights were out, the few remaining flickered in an ugly way that was sure to trigger a migraine if I had to stay in there for any length of time. I knocked on the frosted glass window of the nurse's desk. It was a long moment until it slid open, revealing a disgruntled-looking nurse.

"Can I help you?"

"I'm here to pick up my friend? Jason Sizemore? He came in with kidney stones sometime earlier today," I told her.

The nurse just looked at me. "This hospital is closed."

I sighed. "He's got to be here, his truck is in the parking lot. He's easy to spot. Red-headed dude from Kentucky, wearing a T-shirt with an alien head on it."

She didn't say another word, simply stared at us, her face more blank than confused.

I could see the corridor behind her, leading to the triage area, and spotted a familiar face.

"Boss!" I shouted.

We rushed through the door; the nurse finally spoke. "You can't go in there!"

"Like hell, I can't!"

He was pale, bordering on delirious. There was no IV drip, not even a hospital band. Nothing. He was just lying on the gurney against the wall of the wide hallway.

"It's probably best if you get him out of here."

Katie and I both jumped at the appearance of the doctor. He was a young man, slim and handsome. He had a very competent, calming presence.

"We've done all we can here, but he needs actual care." The doctor indicated the room around us. I noticed the plastic sheeting over the doorways and covered-over windows. "This hospital is closed."

"So we've been told," Katie snarked at him.

"Do I need to sign him out or anything?" I asked.

The doctor laughed. "Nope. Nothing to sign. No one to file it with."

"Well, okay, then." This was all highly unusual. My mom, my aunt, and my godmother were all nurses, I have spent a significant portion of my life around hospitals, and this was all wrong.

Between the two of us, we got my dear, delirious publisher off the gurney.

The doctor sat down on the corner of it and smiled at us, maybe a little flirtatiously. "You two ladies look great, where are you heading?"

"Back to the convention," Katie answered. She batted her eyes. "Wanna join us?"

The doctor looked a little wistful. "I wish I could."

We guided Sizemore back towards the waiting room. "Maybe you should have gotten that doc's number," I said to Katie.

We both looked back, but he was gone.

There was no sign of the nurse at the check-in desk, but the window was still slid open. I could see the mark my fingers had left in the frosted glass, knuckle-shaped streaks in the thick dust. The waiting room chairs were in total disarray, something I hadn't noticed walking in. They too were covered in a layer of dust and grime so thick that I couldn't say what color they were.

"Katie..." I said.

"Just keep walking, don't say another word until we get out of here."

We met the security guard near the door. "I'll be damned..." was all he said.

He stared, open-mouthed, as we hustled Sizemore past him and to the parking lot. Katie helped me get him into the passenger seat of his truck and she went back to her car. She wasted no time backing out of the parking space beside me. As I slid the truck into reverse, I looked up at the hospital. The facade was covered in the last of summer's clinging vines and in between I could see where one tagger after another had left their mark. Only the front windows beside the ER entrance were intact, the rest were boarded up or showed jagged gaps in the grimy glass. Beside me, Sizemore dozed, occasionally making a sound of discomfort.

"I don't know what happened to you in there, Bossman, but you're safe now."

Katie honked a short warning, threatening to leave me behind to find my way back to the hotel on my own. I waved at her and eased the truck out of the lot. She led me out of the crumbling, pot-holed parking lot and back to the hotel as night closed in on us.

In the rear-view mirror, I could see the last flickering fluorescent light in the ER waiting room. It stuttered and strobed, casting wild shadows across the waiting room. It blazed brightly for half a heartbeat then went out, leaving everything behind us lost to darkness.

Chapter 10: Waterfalls

The publishing business will drown you if you're not an adept swimmer. You've got to be adaptable and agile. Your stamina and mental acuity must remain high. Most importantly, you must surround yourself with people who compliment your business and exhibit the hallmarks of success.

👽

For the uninitiated, Gen Con is the Midwest's annual gaming mecca. Approximately 50,000 gaming fans crowd into the Indianapolis Convention Center to play *Magic: The Gathering*, board games, LARPs, RPGs, and virtually anything else you might wish to try. Celebrities and genre luminaries attend and play games with fans: Wil Wheaton, Felicia Day, R.A. Salvatore, and Steve Jackson, to name a few. There's also a strong cosplay community with fantastic costumes that will leave you in awe and bumping into people as you stare in amazement.

Scattered throughout the masses of gamers and cosplayers are people who like books (not that these two things are mutually exclusive). You get a crowd of 50,000 geeks together odds are you're going to find enough science fiction and fantasy readers to make a publisher's investment in table space and four days of time worth their while. I find it certainly does. My first Gen Con proved profitable—from a networking and socializing standpoint, that first Gen Con experience has not been surpassed. If you're a writer, editor, or publisher looking to meet others in the business, you can do worse than Gen Con.

👽

When I attended my first Gen Con, the convention scene had become comfortable and familiar to me. Many things I had encountered and endured: honey baked hams, the blue stuff, the green fairy, kidney stones, and food poisoning. The shy little hillbilly from Big Creek, Kentucky, had grown into a world-class man about town—a man of adventure and the upper echelons of geek society.

Yet... the crowds... the sheer number of major publishers, the throngs of well-known editors and writers intimidated me.

I was lucky to have found McKenzie Johnston Winberry. McKenzie, a smart and driven sixteen-year-old, had contacted me via email about an opportunity to be an intern. She offered to come up to Indianapolis and work the Apex table. We desperately needed the help, so without knowing McKenzie at all, I agreed.

Occasionally, necessity pushes you into your best decisions.

Leading up to Gen Con, Maurice had rattled on about Monica Valentinelli. *She's the coolest. I just had to meet her.*

"Monica might be the coolest person you'll ever meet," he asserted.

"So you say," I said.

"No, you're being obtuse. Don't be obtuse. Monica is the coolest person you'll ever meet."

"But you just said she *might* be the coolest person. Now you're speaking in absolutes?"

"She'll introduce us to all the top hiring editors."

"Meh." I had plenty of work on my plate. I knew enough famous editors to fill a short bus.

"She'll get us invited into all the best parties. She's a writer, an editor, a raconteur!"

"Okay."

Maurice scowled at me. "Why are you so obtuse?"

Honestly, I couldn't wait to meet Monica. She sounded like

a resourceful and intelligent person. People like Monica have high utility scores for companies like Apex.

When the first day of Gen Con started, McKenzie shared her goal with me: the Apex table would have a huge day in sales. Money! I liked this kid already. She and I high-fived and performed a ritualistic money chant. Her enthusiasm was contagious. I applied my best smile and forced myself to be witty and likable. Today would be the day I would sell mass quantities of Apex books!

Thirty minutes into our first day, with many people approaching the table and leaving without making a purchase, it became obvious to me that I was a problem. My face expressed financial desperation. McKenzie's face expressed sincere friendliness. We both agreed that she would do all the talking from thereon.

McKenzie also had retail experience, having worked the counter at her family's business. She also had an eye-twinkling charm and laid-back nature that people were comfortable around. Often, McKenzie would stop passers-by with a simple and direct "Hello" and draw them to our table. My greetings often solicited a curt nod and swift change in direction. McKenzie's broad smile created a set of adorable dimples that pulled in customers like aggressive black birds to a feeder. She also had the ability to upsell like a pro, a skill I've never possessed.

Dollar signs flashed in my eyes. This kid was going to make me rich!

During a lull of foot traffic, I asked her when she had picked up her retail talents—in particular, saying the right things to get the guys to spend more.

"What do you mean?" she asked, puzzled.

My face reddened. "Um, uh, you know, with the smiles and the talking."

"Oh, you mean being social and friendly?"

I nodded. I *think* that's what I meant.

"Basic retail strategies. You should give it a try."

"I do. I did. I smile and they run."

McKenzie raised an eyebrow. "Oh. That was a smile?"

"What did you think I was doing?"

McKenzie paused. "I don't want to say."

Apex was having its best day ever until The Carnival Barker arrived.

The guy goes down in Sizemore Recorded History as one of the most annoying individuals I've had the displeasure of encountering, even with my third superpower's way of attracting annoying people to me. It is beyond my reckoning as to how this fellow has not been kicked in the gonads, repeatedly, by frustrated fellow dealers. There is a shortlist of unspoken commandments of polite vending: don't socialize in front of another's table, don't intrude on a fellow vendor's area, and so on. This guy broke the most important rule of all: don't steal another's customer.

I had returned from lunch, and McKenzie was having a conversation with a potential customer discussing the virtues of *Dark Faith*. A loud voice originating from the table next to ours erupted across the vendor hall.

"Young man, do you enjoy tales of adventure, daring-do, and heroic feats?"

The Barker stood rigidly upright. He wore white pants and a red-and-white striped shirt. In his hand he held out a book.

The young man looked up, confused. He looked to McKenzie, then back to the Barker. "Yes?" he croaked.

"Of course you do, son. We all do. Even the pretty young lady you're speaking with loves daring-do. Add a spice of mysticism, magic, yes that's right people, I said *magic*, a young hero wanting to make a difference in the world, a pulse-pounding plot, and you'll discover why *Above the Others* has picked up 137, that's right I said 137, 5-star Amazon reviews."

"That's… that's a lot," the kid mumbled.

"I always say there's nothing better than having a taste of

the real deal yourself before you spend your hard-earned cash." Here the Carnival Barker stepped up and shoved a copy of *Above the Others* into the guy's hand.

I was stunned. McKenzie was stunned. The young man in front of our table was stunned. The Barker's ribald attitude did not sit well with me.

Finally, with a zombie-like gait, the young man walked over and started flipping through *Above the Others* and stood in front of the Barker's table.

"Wait," McKenzie called out, dismayed.

This went on for four long days.

I complained to the vendor hall manager.

"Oh, that's Robert. He's been to every Gen Con for the last ten years. Everybody complains about him."

"And you still have him back?" I asked.

The vendor hall manager looked at me over a set of half-moon lenses that rested on her nose. "He pays, he stays."

Greedy bastards.

I whined to other vendors. They were sympathetic, but offered little succor.

"You're the new guy, and they always put the new guy next to Robert. It's like a rite of passage or something."

Even in the world of geekdom, there's hazing.

My frustration mounted during Gen Con's lengthy vendor hours. I became surly and grumpy and in an ill mood to socialize and network. Maurice had talked Monica into coming to the vendor hall after it closed for a meet and greet. I would have rather performed a meet-and-greet with Robert and a baseball bat.

Presently, I stood outside the vendor hall with Maurice, McKenzie, and Jerry Gordon awaiting the arrival of Monica Valentinelli. Maurice behaved giddily. Jerry engaged in conversation with McKenzie. I pouted.

"Here she comes," Maurice said. He performed a final check of his red pin-striped suit and tie.

"You're pretty enough," I said.

Maurice looked over to me. "Sizemore, stop slouching. You look like a sullen six-year-old."

Whatever.

Monica approached, accompanied by an entourage of geeks that surrounded her like a head of state. She made a joke I did not hear, but the entourage laughed in unison.

She stopped and her gaze fell on us. Monica gave Maurice and Jerry each a warm, familiar embrace.

"Monica," Maurice said, "I want you to meet Jason Sizemore, owner of Apex Publications."

I nodded and shook her hand. Her cold, appraising eyes reminded me of the way Professor Snape stared down at Harry Potter in the movies.

"And this is McKenzie Johnston, Apex Intern and Keeper of the Sizemore."

McKenzie and Monica shook hands.

"You need a keeper?" Monica asked me. I watched as she registered my black Apex T-shirt, baggy Levis, and tennis shoes. "You look innocuous enough."

"He has a way of finding trouble," Maurice said. "For reasons I'd rather not bore you with."

Monica frowned. "I think the reasons are because he's naïve and out of his element."

Maurice chuckled. "You *do* know the reason."

My pouting grew in magnitude.

Monica placed a hand on Maurice's shoulder. "I have bad news. I won't be able to join you for dinner."

Maurice looked crestfallen.

"But I heard that Matt Forbeck was looking for you. I will text him and hook you guys up," Monica added.

An hour later, the four of us met with Matt outside the convention hall. I found Matt to be personable, friendly, and an all-around good guy. He invited the group to join him at a local bar where he had a private room reserved. An enthusiastic cheer went up.

"Lead on," Jerry said.

My plus-one was sixteen years old. I couldn't take her in the bar. But I didn't want to miss hanging out with Matt Forbeck. He had promised free booze!

McKenzie could see the ongoing struggle playing out on my face. Being the eternal sweetheart that she is, she instructed me to go on with the fellas.

I refused. "No way. I'm not leaving you alone at Gen Con."

"Don't be silly. There are plenty of people my age hanging out. I'll find a game to join back in the convention center. When you're done, call me and we'll figure out what to do next."

I *want* to believe that I hesitated for a long, long time before making my decision. It would make me feel less of an asshole.

I gave McKenzie twenty bucks and promised her I wouldn't be long. An hour, tops.

And off I went, leaving the sixteen-year-old standing on the corner of a busy street.

The special reserved room was painted red and shaped like a square. A cloth covered the entrance. Bench seats lined the three walls, and a group of nervous writers sat staring at one another. After a long wait, we were served free drinks. Several times I was questioned on the whereabouts of my nice intern, prompting me to explain that she wasn't of legal drinking age and that I left her on the street. I drank my guilt away.

A couple of hours later, a bar manager entered our den and explained that a mistake had been made. The room we occupied needed to be cleared out immediately, that it had been reserved for another party. As we exited, a group of younger, better dressed men laughed and took our places. I think we had been replaced by someone more popular! Also, our free booze card had been revoked.

Annoyed and embarrassed, I decided to leave and search for my intern.

It took nearly an hour, but I eventually found her on a street corner having an animated conversation with a homeless guy. If I recall, they were discussing Kant philosophy. What kid does that?

Guilt gnawed at me. I was a horrible boss and a worse friend. I was an irresponsible adult who had left a sixteen-year-old alone on the streets in a crowded, strange city.

I apologized then. I apologize now. McKenzie, being the eternal sweetheart she is, forgave me. Of course, she also plays the "You abandoned me" card to get whatever favor she needs from me. From her perspective, I am told, it worked out well.

👽

The next morning, McKenzie informed me that Apex was declaring war on the Carnival Barker. She wore a jagged floral skirt and a nice brown leather corset. Her hair was done up in curls and tied back with cute flowery clips. She looked quite adorable.

"If you're dressing up fancy to sell books, you know it's not necessary. How about wearing your Apex T-shirt?"

McKenzie cast me a scornful look. "Dummy. This isn't for you or for Apex. I wear this at all the cons."

"You're going to give the teenage boys heart palpitations."

"I've not killed anybody yet," she said, and off we went.

The Barker had arrived early and was already busy annoying people. McKenzie worked on preparing our table. I decided to have a chat with Robert. I'm not shy about addressing problems head on.

"Hello."

"Young man," he prompted, "do you enjoy tales—"

I waved him quiet. "Robert. I'm right next to you. I've heard your spiel about 350 times. I don't want your book."

He smiled. His teeth were bright white and straight like

painted Popsicle sticks. "Sorry, fella, I start talking about my books and everything else around me fades to black."

"I want to talk to you about something."

"Sure."

"Do you mind not harassing potential buyers when they're in front of my table?"

Robert looked over and saw McKenzie leaning over, placing books on our table. A rueful look crossed his face. "Oh... I see your sales strategy." He winked.

"No! She's sixteen."

McKenzie Johnston Winberry
selling like a boss

He cocked an eyebrow and titled his head askance.

"Forget it. Have a good day."

Soon after, Robert went about his business of selling a lot more books than McKenzie and me.

Later that morning, I spotted Hickory Adams shuffling his way toward us.

"Quick, let me hide under the table!"

"I think not," McKenzie said. "I'm wearing a skirt!"

"You can stand!"

"No. My feet need a break."

"Mr. Sizemore."

My face fell forward in resignation.

"Hello, Mr. Adams. Having a good con?"

"Not in particular. This was advertised as a gaming convention. Not a single person here knows how to play pinochle or euchre."

"These are geeky gamers. I don't think they play traditional card games."

"Are you saying you're too good to play pinochle?"

I stared at Hickory. He wore a set of glasses with large, tan lenses along with a bomber jacket. The vendor hall had to be close to 80 degrees. I don't know how he could stand it in such a coat.

"I'm not saying anything like that," I said.

"I heard you with my two ears. That's the problem with guys like you. No respect of your elders."

McKenzie, sensing my rising anger, interrupted. "Mr. Adams, would you like to buy a book? We have a great new anthology—"

"So this is what it's come to, Mr. Sizemore? Having comely young lasses sell for you?"

"Not at all!"

"How old is this one? Not a day older than thirty-five I bet. She's a whippersnapper!"

I guffawed. "No, McKenzie is sixteen."

Hickory blinked at me. "You, sir, have no shame."

"She's just my intern, Mr. Adams."

"I've finished a new book. Would you like to hear about it?"

I looked over at McKenzie. She shrugged.

"Okay," I said.

"In the near future, our President Obama has declared martial law over West Point. Our proud young servicemen usurp our dictator-in-chief and install a clone of Ronald Reagan to lead the country."

"Wow." I couldn't think of anything else to say.

"For once, I agree with you, Mr. Sizemore. The novel is great."

"Have you *ever* read an Apex title?"

Hickory frowns at me. "You're right. My book is too good for Apex."

"That's exactly it," I agreed.

Sometime in the afternoon, Maurice and Jerry sauntered to our table. Maurice took one look at McKenzie, then at me.

"Really, Sizemore?"

"What? It's what she wanted to wear!"

"Right."

Jerry shrugged. "Whatever works, right?" I couldn't tell if he was being accusatory or if he was being sincere.

McKenzie shut the book she was reading and looked up. "Oh, hi, guys!"

"How are sales?" Jerry asked.

"Not bad, but they would be better if it weren't for the bozo next to us." I pointed at Robert the Huckster doing his song and dance to an entranced geek in a black T-shirt.

"Can you run the table alone for a few minutes? I need a break." McKenzie asked.

I waved McKenzie away. As she exited our booth, Monica Valentinelli and her entourage of sycophants appeared.

Looking directly at me, Monica said, "Hello, McKenzie."

"Hi! Nice to see you again, Monica." McKenzie acted oblivious to the look I was receiving.

My intern walked away and disappeared into the crowd.

"Sizemore. You have got to be kidding me." Monica turned to Maurice. "You want me to *work* with this guy?"

Maurice shrugged, offering no words of support.

"Anyway, I got everybody tickets to the White Wolf party at the club tonight. Well there's not a ticket for Jason's booth babe." Monica let the comment trail off with tart judgment.

"That's okay, she's too young, anyway," I said.

"No kidding?" Monica responded.

"No kidding. And she's not a booth babe."

The noise from the table next to mine grew louder. "Adventure! Mayhem!"

Monica flipped through some Apex books while making idle talk. "Well, these aren't half bad."

"Thank you."

"If I decide to publish with you, what sort of dress code will you require?"

"None," I stammered. "I don't make anybody dress like anything!"

"Goddamn right you don't," Monica said. Then she smiled at me. "I'm kidding, Sizemore. Can you tell when people are joking with you?"

I was flustered. Of course I know when people are joking with me. I'm a smart ass by design. "Of course!"

"Good. I'll remember that before I make merry with you again."

The crowd in front of the Apex booth dispersed and made way to a growing group in front of Robert's booth. In a matter of a few minutes, I stood alone.

An hour later, McKenzie returned, and she and I resumed our hard work. By the time the vending hall closed two days later, Apex had sold a record amount of books for a convention event.

Via scuttlebutt, I heard an outrageous four-digit number that represented the Carnival Barker's take from Gen Con.

It was the Saturday evening of Gen Con, the night of the White Wolf party. McKenzie had been ensconced safely at Jerry's house. Maurice, Jerry, and I stood together, clutching drink tokens. We watched revelers dance and move about.

Have you ever watched *Law & Order* where the cops go into a dance club to have an unannounced sit-down with some mid-level crime lord? The White Wolf party was like that, except filled with geeks instead of the usual cadre of drunken dude bros and sweaty young women. An elevated dance floor adorned the center of the club. At each of the floor's vertices, a cage had been installed around a metal pole. Each cage had a door and an accompanying gyrating attractive young woman.

This was my first time inside a dance club of any sort, if you don't count high school dances. Here I felt like a smothering guppy dying on the surface of a scorching desert stone. I cashed in my drink token on an old fashioned and spent way too much money on four or five more. Eventually, the alcohol worked its magic. The nervousness eased away.

The club had a second floor. (Just like the ones on television!) Oversized loveseats and couches lining the walls were crowded with VIPs and young women brought in as party adornment by our hosts. Maurice, Jerry, and I clung to Monica downstairs, networking and gossiping with other writers.

In the midst of a Monica story regarding some ill-behaving editor—are there any other types?—she stopped and looked at me. "Sizemore, did you spill something on your shirt."

I laughed. If I had learned anything in my limited interactions with Monica it was that she liked to joke around.

"No, really. Don't you feel it?"

And as soon as she said it, I felt it. A warm liquid trickled down my sleeve. I stepped back and looked up. Directly above me, a woman smiled and waved down. She wore a tight red blouse and a short, short black skirt. From my angle I could see that she lacked the modest measure of an undergarment. Shocked, I jumped away and then it dawned on me.

Noooooo, I thought. I had received a baptism of an unholy nature.

The woman wasn't holding a cup. But a warm liquid had fallen on my shirt.

I looked up again. The woman had disappeared.

My stomach lurched at the thought, at the possibility.

I made an abrupt exit and rushed back to my hotel room.

"Jason," you'll ask. "Do you *really* think a random woman peed on you at a dance club?"

I'll answer "No. Don't be silly."

I try to be optimistic. I analyze the angles. Lay out the realities. I've concluded that most likely somebody had spilled his or her drink. The contents fell over the edge of the second floor, warmed to body temperature, and splattered me. I was in the wrong place at the wrong time. I was the victim of an innocent party foul. The lady above me saw me peering up her skirt, labelled me a pervert, and went somewhere else to stand.

Occam's razor, right?

Here's an important tip if you decide to venture into writing, editing, or publishing. Surround yourself with successful friends. You'll be faced with an incredible amount of doubters, with assholes who care only of themselves, and random people who simply want to piss on your parade. Having people around like Maurice, Monica, Jerry, and McKenzie to offer their assistance and experience in times of need will keep your mental state healthy and your publishing career on track.

The Case of the Mysterious Warm Splatter

Eyewitness Rebuttal

Monica Valentinelli

Monica, would you like to write a rebuttal? It'll give you a chance to set the record straight just in case my memory wasn't as great as I thought it was."

"Um… So, in a sense, you're asking me to *argue* with you? In writing?"

"Yeah, it'll be fun!"

This is why Jason Sizemore is my friend. For, of all the pieces I've ever been asked to write, he requests I pen what comes as naturally to me as rolling my eyes—something that would take about fifteen minutes of my time[18] depending upon caffeine levels, given how fast I type.

Currently, I am writing this rebuttal on the eve of Fish Fool's following a terribly long winter, the submission of a Victorian-era satirical piece that required more commas than I would ever deign to use in a 3,000-word short story on a bad day,[19] and without my usual levels of hyper-caffeination. I am, as you would imagine, hiding from the merciless sunlight (and my cats) with a glass of whisky lemonade at my left, a pile of deadlines at my right, and an art piece titled *The Ghastlytomb Dungeons*, whose monsters glare at me while I type. Combined, my mental state is currently scaling toward mildly neurotic, as I am also praying to rid myself of the Poe-esque prose that has infected my poor brain like the catchy tune *Lo Pan Style*, yet another iteration of Psy's *Gangnam Style*—three years later!

---

[18] Thirty minutes if you count revisions. Of course, this may be a slight exaggeration, but you get the idea. **(Monica Valentinelli)**

[19] Footnotes, on the other hand… **(Monica Valentinelli)**

If you would indulge my eccentricities for a moment, before I begin to scold Jason on his less-than-desirable recollection of our first meeting, I'd like to mention that he did manage to get one thing right. Okay, two—*if* you count the fact that Professor Severus Snape is my spirit animal, for Snape represents the careful and reserved persona I have had to adapt when dealing with science fiction and fantasy types.

Please, I beg you dear Reader. Do not leap to the worst possible conclusion (This is not Twitter, after all!) and allow me to explain. No, seriously... put away your vorpal swords and the One Ring. It'll be *okay*.

What Jason did get right, is that my natural state of being is to connect one person to another. This is a side effect that has occurred due to my habit of collecting stories. I love them dearly and, as people (including many writers, apparently) often tell the best stories, I enjoy talking to a *lot* of people. However, I am also a writer who suffers from quite a few neuroses—like many of you, I'd imagine. That, coupled with the fact that my superpower is Perfect Timing,[20] means whenever I'm out in the general public, I'm....

Oh, who am I kidding, anyway? There's no rhyme or reason to my madness, because I don't think about the "rules" of how to interact with other people in publishing, other than to err on the side of common decency and manners.[21] (If you believe that there is a secret hierarchy that determines the worth of a human being based on [insert your preferred criteria here], then baby, I have a share of Sealand to sell you.) As an exceptionally lazy person when it comes to social interaction, namely because "the rules" bore me to tears, I find that caring about all that nonsense seems like a lot of *work*. Treat people as well as they can be treated, and the rest will sort itself out.

---

[20] I have the unfortunate habit of cracking jokes that turn out to be true. Once, I was at an airport and joked about a woman setting off the alarm because she had a metal plate in her head. She did. **(Monica Valentinelli)**

[21] For example, never get into a fight with a Sicilian when death is on the line, and try to avoid pitching to an agent in the bathroom. **(Monica Valentinelli)**

Yes, my secret is out. I really am that simple,[22] and this is important background information to share for this rebuttal. Be a good person, tell a story, grab a drink (non-alcoholic included), and leave the encounter changed for the better. Only, the challenge for me is that my experience at SF&F cons thus far has been no shortage of pissing people off for either asking for an autograph (No, I'm really *not* kidding on that last.), or not following the rules of diva/Devo worship. This is through no fault of anyone else's and, sadly, my ignorance of the rules will never change for, like midicholorians,[23] I do not understand them. In my defense, I have been through a fair amount of strife, and the only real fear I have while navigating a convention is that someone will be left alone in a sea of people, and not by choice. To me, coming away from a social engagement with a feeling of uncomfortable angst is the exact opposite of what conventions were designed for. I prefer to meet new people, connect whenever possible, and then laugh about all our faux pas[24] like old friends the next time we meet at a con. Doesn't everyone?

To continue setting the stage for The Case of the Mysterious Warm Splatter, I'd also like to explain how I was introduced to Maurice Broaddus. Prior to meeting Jason, my friend Lucien Soulban[25] told me I need to meet the "Sinister Minister."[26] This, too, is important for context, for the way Lucien promoted this particular individual gave me the sense that the Sinister Minister was a short call away from a

---

[22] For those of you who know me personally and are reading this statement, I suspect you're laughing right now. **(Monica Valentinelli)**

[23] Yes, like midichlorians, the "rules" have been explained to me. I understand what the literal definition is, but semantically, I'd much rather be watching grass grow than waste one second on caring about that crap. **(Monica Valentinelli)**

[24] Of all the stories in science fiction and fantasy land, unfortunately, tales of the faux pas are so common I fear they've become their own trope. **(Monica Valentinelli)**

[25] Lucien Soulban is a genre writer who has written novels, games, and short stories. I adore him! **(Monica Valentinelli)**

[26] Quite possibly, the absolute best and scariest name for an individual I had ever heard. I imagined he'd be eight feet tall and shoot cross-shaped arrows from his eyes. Or wrestle! **(Monica Valentinelli)**

Hollywood movie. Not only was he an excellent dresser, mind you, he was a popular blogger *destined* for stardom, a slayer of demonic forces with his righteous pen in one hand, and his crucifix in another.

Of course, I'm talking about Maurice Broaddus, whom I am also proud to call my friend.

Maurice was reserved and focused the first time I met him, when he interviewed me oh-shit-*how*-many-years-ago. I remember him being very professional yet careful not to get *too* personal, but I was curious about him. By this I mean: here was an individual marrying horror with religion in a way that causes a lot of *horror-writers-are-Satanic* types to raise eyebrows and/or picket bookstores. He had to have "the" story to tell, and I needed to know it.

As most conventions like Gen Con go for me, however, I got busy and distracted. I often joke about how multi-media cons are so much easier than literary events, because if you don't like someone you can always find something fun[27] to do. Maurice was happy to introduce me to Jason and McKenzie, and I thought they were, to borrow a word I think is fucking fantastic: lovely. To this day, I swear by my deep and profound love for Freddie Mercury that I had no idea McKenzie was *that* young. Booth babe? Please, Mr. Sizemore, do not offend my genteel nature so. What I was worried about was whether or not the newbies to this show had enough to do, and that they were having a good time despite the crowds.

However....

I must take a moment to admit why Jason felt I was channeling Professor Snape. I can come across colder than Boston's winter of 2014-2015, for despite all my boisterous hand gestures,[28] I am still

---

[27] I now understand why there's a contingent of writers who prefer BarCon to the main event. Perhaps many things can be forgiven when one's blood alcohol level reaches catastrophic proportions, for even those who don't drink could certainly fake it. **(Monica Valentinelli)**

[28] Yes, it's really okay. I am *that* Italian, and had to rid myself of hugs and smiling at people long ago. File under: things that really freak people out! **(Monica Valentinelli)**

an introvert uncomfortable around people I don't know very well. I manage okay, apparently, because, of all the characters I should be associated with, I could do worse than Severus,[29] to be sure, especially since my mechanism to compensate for my neuroses is to do the exact opposite of what most people might expect. In other words, I default to my natural state of sarcasm. After all, if Jason might survive a well-or-poorly timed barb from yours truly, then surely I'm safe from being exiled to the Unacceptable Geek corner, an act that would make Grumpy Cat cry.

Now that I have done my duty as a writer and bared a piece of my soul for posterity's sake, hopefully my rebuttals of the "booth babe" and "Snape" references were effective in a way that has satisfied you, so you'll no doubt recommend a copy of *For Exposure* to your family and friends.[30] This, oddly enough, means that it's now time to regale you with the story of the White Wolf[31] party where the mysterious splatter took place, for Jason's version is certainly not how *I* remember it.

Picture if you will, an industrial warehouse that is unassuming on the outside, but transformed temporarily to contain all manner of Goths, game designers, writers, fans, and gamers on the inside. Like many clubs, it was dark and the slick floor was designed by a brilliant scientist so it could be mopped up quickly in case of spillage. There was a second floor, a balcony for the DJ,[32] and a pair of birdcages that hung down from the ceiling on chains. In these cages, professional

---

[29] Maleficent has the absolute best name of any villainess. I also like Lady Death, because mortality is quite the bitch, if it weren't for the character's rendering. **(Monica Valentinelli)**

[30] Jason forced me to write this. I'm so sorry. **(Monica Valentinelli)**

[31] White Wolf is the company that produced fiction and role-playing games like *Vampire: the Masquerade* which celebrated its 20th anniversary in 2011. The company has since merged with CCP, creators of MMOs like *Eve Online*, and the RPG properties are being licensed to Onyx Path Publishing. **(Monica Valentinelli)**

[32] Justin Achilli was DJ'ing that evening. He had his work cut out for him, since the age range was 21-65. **(Monica Valentinelli)**

dancers set the mood for the crowd, and danced to the beat of the music.

I'll get to them a little later.

Unlike Jason, I must confess that this was definitely *not* my first party, and I felt it was pretty tame by comparison to the wildness of my youth.[33] My youth, of course, hadn't quite ended yet—but Facebook and people's tendencies to record everything from the size of their hernias to their preferred brand of breakfast cereal was not a "thing" when I was having fun.[34] Cell phones, however, were in vogue at that time, and it's important to mention that we all had them at the party.

On to my rebuttal, and the thrilling conclusion of The Case of the Mysterious Splatter!

Let me think for a moment. So where were we? Jason, Maurice, and several other people, including myself, were standing beneath the second floor just as he had claimed. The second floor was not a solid plane, but a metal grate, which meant that a pen could drop right through a hole and land on the first level partiers below. The dimly lit bar was crowded, so it was hard to see across the room if you weren't right beneath a spotlight, and getting drinks was a process that required standing in line for a half an hour or so. Due to the music's volume and chatter of the crowd, it was also very hard to hear.[35]

Despite the noise, we shared many stories, and I distinctly recall one part of my conversation with Jason: I repeatedly told him *not* to look directly above us.

"What do you mean? Is this what they do at parties?" I remember Jason asking me.

"Wait, what? You've never been to a party before?" I'm sure I had an involuntary reaction to this, of the *why-didn't-*

---

[33] I'm as pure as the driven snow. I swear it! **(Monica Valentinelli)**

[34] See also: why I really, really feel for kids these days. **(Monica Valentinelli)**

[35] My twenty-year old self is crying a little bit. Right now. **(Monica Valentinelli)**

Maurice-tell-me variety. "Never mind that. Just don't look up, okay?"

"Well, why? I'm askin'."

"Just don't."

"Well, why?" he repeated with that Kentuckian drawl of his. "You gotta tell me why I can't look up, otherwise I'm gonna. You can't just tell me not to look up and not explain it."[36]

"Fine, Jason, then by all means. Be my guest." At this point, I was frustrated that our exchange was more complicated than a George R.R. Martin plot. "What the hell? Go ahead. Look up."

"Well, now I can't look up just 'cause you told me to. Seriously, Monica. Why can't I look up?"

And then Jason did the one thing that Should Not Be Done. He *smirked* at me. I still remember that Cheshire grin, and how he swayed in time with the music. The signs were unmistakable: Jason was trying to fuck with me. Here I was attempting to have a serious conversation with him, and he felt it was all one big joke—despite the fact that I was really trying to save him from bleaching his eyeballs!

"Well, Jason, of *course* I wouldn't want you to look up knowing your reputation," I said, deciding to play to his vanity. "You see, there's a really attractive woman up there who might not realize the dangers of being on the second floor in a miniskirt. I mean, she could be into that sort of thing, but you're probably the type of guy who'd want to save her from embarrassment. Wouldn't you?"

I couldn't have timed his response better. When Jason looked up—I kid you not—some beer spilled onto his shirt. At the exact same moment, his eyes widened and he stared blankly at me. I don't think he blinked for a full minute. Then, he slowly backed away from the group in a moment

---

[36] Monica nails my curiosity and stubbornness in one paragraph. She needs to work on the drawl. **(Jason Sizemore)**

so uncomfortable, it was as if he'd just won a Hugo award and was told to "hold that rocket steady."[37]

"Monica, why didn't you warn me? WHY?"

I smiled, and said nothing. Yes, oh yes, Jason did look up to that second floor and saw right through the holes in the grate to witness an unfortunate sight—despite the fact that I had repeatedly (and vigorously) told him *not* to. You see, when Jason looked up he did not see an attractive woman or her thong, but a group of friendly Scots who were wearing their kilts in the traditional fashion.[38]

Yep, I'm evil. Eeeeeeeeevil!

Now that I've revealed the truth behind Jason's colorful rendition of what he convinced himself that stain might be,[39] I must offer a rebuttal to another point, which was stashed away in his professions of innocence.

My rebuttal isn't about what Jason said about the party, it's about what he *didn't* say. Sadly, I have already indulged you with my Monica-isms to the point where you're probably wondering who this crazy person is,[40] but before I go? Remember those girls-in-cages I mentioned earlier?

One of the dancers was dressed all in black; her two-piece costume was a pair of hot pants and a bustier. The hot pants had a series of bouncy tassels on them that were well-paced to accentuate the gyration of her hips. These dangly, rhythmic balls proved to be a powerful magnet that totally and utterly mesmerized Sizemore and the Sinister Minister, and they were

---

[37] After Jason dumped me as a date for the Hugos, I had a nightmare about what would happen if I ever won one. I am secretly grateful he didn't, for I would never be able to live down whatever faux pas I'd be sure to commit at that ceremony. **(Monica Valentinelli)**

[38] Apologies for my lack of description here, but I could not bring myself to write the details of Jason's unfortunate view. And it's not the Scots' fault, for they are lovely people! **(Monica Valentinelli)**

[39] Editors. I tell ya! **(Monica Valentinelli)**

[40] I don't like talking about myself or my work as much as Jason and Maurice do, that's for sure. **(Monica Valentinelli)**

attracted to them like a reader at a Neil Gaiman sighting.[41] While everybody else was keeping their distance, having conversations, and letting the girls dance, these two were parked in front of that shaky bum with their cell phones at the ready to take video of the spectacle and digitally archive it.

Sadly, all rebuttals must end eventually,[42] and I must conclude The Case of the Mysterious Splatter by sharing these final thoughts: I have no idea what has become of said video. What happened *after* that, however, is a secret I shall take to my grave—forevermore.

Thus my time in *For Exposure*,[43] like the conventions Jason and I attend together, must draw to a close. I hereby verify that all you've read in this argumentative piece is true to my understanding, and because Jason is my friend, if I'm ever pressed to testify in a court of law (or before his lovely family) I shall plead my case with the wise words of my ancestors: I know nothing, I see nothing, I hear nothing.

P.S.: Jason, the Duchess of Montana says "Hi."

---

[41] See? SEE! I *have* been to a science fiction and fantasy convention! **(Monica Valentinelli)**

[42] Agatha Christie would be proud, I think. **(Monica Valentinelli)**

[43] Bonus book title name drop! **(Monica Valentinelli)**

"If I have seen further, it is by standing on the shoulders of giants."

—Isaac Newton

Greatness requires an enormous investment of time. The journalist Malcolm Gladwell describes the "10,000 hour rule" in his book *Outliers*. Gladwell makes a claim (based on a study by the Swedish psychologist K. Anders Ericsson) that it takes 10,000 hours of practice or experience to become a master of one field or specific task.

Early on I decided that serving 10,000 hours would take too long on my own. I have a life to live! To help me leapfrog up the publishing/editing experience chart, over the past ten years I've enlisted many smart, driven individuals to work for Apex Publications. By my calculations, we're nearing 100,000 hours.

At this point, I feel secure in describing myself as a megamaster of the small press.

Those who have helped me reach 100,000 hours of mastery deserve a small measure of recognition. While I don't have the space to mention everybody who has chipped in, I'd like to share the names, accomplishments, and contributions of a few memorable past and current editors.

Gill Ainsworth

If I'm the Lord Creator of Apex Publications, then Gill Ainsworth is its Queen Mother. She served as the Apex Publications' senior editor for over five years. She is an expert grammarian and copy editor. A perfect person to have around in every manner of speaking but one: she's British.

Don't get me wrong. Some of my best friends are British! But Gill's manner of speaking (and editing) caused, at times, difficulties with our decidedly American Apex fan base. Most famously, a well-respected and popular review journal reviewed *The Apex Book of World SF*, which Gill edited. The reviewer explicitly stated that the occurrence of the word "whilst" throughout the text ruined the entire anthology for him. He instructed his readers to avoid our book.

Writers who wrote in American English often expressed confusion with some of Gill's edits. "Who put the letter U in all my words?" was a common complaint. Breaking Gill of this habit took a bit of effort.

Gill, sadly, moved on to other interests, such as European beer and vacations. She last communicated with me from her summer home in Crete, where she was enjoying a mimosa whilst being fanned by an "island boy."

Deb Taber

When I think of Deb Taber, I think of her many part-time jobs with a laundry list of small companies. The most memorable of these was for a business named Horse Source or something similar. The first time she emailed me from her Horse Source account, I was caught by surprise. For a split second, I thought the email domain read "whore sauce." Of course I had to tell her, and like a pair of goofball grade school students, we have giggled about whore sauce for almost a decade.

Deb, to her credit, matured into a fantastic author and editor. She released a novel through the well-respected independent publisher Aqueduct Press and landed a full-time editing position at a major New York publisher.

I, on the other hand, am still giggling over whore sauce.

Amanda Dailey-Weaver

One of my weaknesses as a businessman is in the area of marketing. It's always been a struggle, and I suspect it will always be. In the early years of Apex, Amanda played an important role by helping bring eyes to our brand.

Amanda functioned as the de facto leader of an informal Apex Street Team. She travelled to a lot of fan events, promoting the digest everywhere she went. She helped with our first few room parties and at several Apex-related bookstore signings.

During one fateful conversation, we decided that the notion of "sex sells" was true and viable even in book publishing (Hey, I warned you that I suck at marketing) and we should create promotional Apex posters featuring Amanda wearing an Apex T-shirt. She and her aunt took some shots and mailed them to me, asking for my opinion.

In the pictures, Amanda was dressed in the Apex T-shirt as planned and not a whole lot else. My opinion was "Wow!" but, either due to cold feet or a moment of better judgment, I didn't think it was a good idea to produce Apex pinup posters. Amanda confided that there was already a demand for the poster and that she knew of many college students who would hang them in their dorms and apartments. If I'm anything, I'm a greedy bastard, so I surreptitiously had a few hundred printed and sold them for 20 bucks apiece, sharing the profits with Amanda.

The posters sold out in a week. Even now, I am occasionally asked about the availability of the Amanda poster. I have one in my private stash of Apex memorabilia, but I'm not selling it.

Jerry Gordon[44]

In a swirling sea of angst and anxiety, Jerry Gordon is a beacon of calm.

Any stressed businessman needs a person like Jerry. He's my punching bag, of sorts, for all the venting, swearing, and bragging that running a publishing company generates. After hearing all my ranting nonsense, he collates the data, sorts fact from fiction, and presents invaluable wise counsel.

Jerry is also one of the few humans who can read my mood and mental state. He's been known to warn off writers from

---

[44] Jerry's nickname is "Loquacious Motherfucker". It is a pseudonym of love. (Jason Sizemore)

making an untimely story pitch ("No, no, no. If you value your life, come back later."), redirect my wrath from innocent victims, and keep my redhead, redneck temper in check.

Without Jerry, I would probably be covered head to toe by Apex alien head tattoos and ensconced deep in the halls of a mental institution.

Jerry is also a software developer. He's a great resource when I need a second opinion regarding technical issues. Jerry's utility score is off the charts.

Lesley Conner[45]

Every company has an outward facing boss as perceived by the public and the true boss known within the walls of the company. While I might be seen as Mr. Apex, the truth is, Lesley is the gasoline that keeps the motor roaring. She's the lube to the crankshafts. She is the brake pads of the runaway train known as Apex.

I'm the most disorganized person I know. When I was younger, this wasn't a problem. I had a sharp mind and could remember most scheduled appointments and dates, and where I left important documents and bills in the junk pile known as my office. Now that I'm older, I don't remember most everything. In contrast, Lesley is the most organized person I know. She's the anal retentive perfectionist to my irresponsible messy slacker. I picture her home office organized with rows and rows of dust-free shelves that run on and on, to a point far off on the horizon. Like the sterile archival bunkers of government secrets you'll see portrayed on television.

We work great together. Two puzzle pieces that are a perfect occupational match.

---

[45] Look, I work pretty closely with Jason on a daily basis. There are plenty of times when I'm certain he is just flying blindly by the seat of his pants. When that happens, I create a spreadsheet to keep everything organized. That's what we do. It's our process. And you know what? So far it has worked pretty damn well. So yeah, there are lots of times I wonder if Jason knows what in the hell he's doing, but I also know that in the end he'll figure it out. In the meantime, I make him a spreadsheet. **(Lesley Conner)**

Lesley also sees to my mental stability in the absence of Jerry Gordon. She often describes this as her favorite bit of Apex work. I always thought she enjoyed being a friend, proud of her ability to function effectively in the role. However, in one of my more lucid moments, it occurred to me that I'm the victim of a long con where she gains total control of my brain.

What she wants with my brain is anybody's guess. Jason Sizemore and Albert Einstein: two people famous for having their brains stolen! Whatever she wants to do with it is fine with me. Lesley Conner gets shit done.

Jettie Necole

When you're the king of a kingdom, you need somebody to work as quality control. Quality control covers a broad spectrum of tasks ranging from "Hey, does this press release come across as obnoxious?" to "Do I look hot in this Facebook selfie?"

I call Jettie Necole the Apex Publications Director of Quality Assurance. Not to her face. Only in my mind and in this book. When seeking help from talented friends and you pay only in exposure, it is important to not let them know the magnitude of their contributions. Otherwise, you're looking at having to open your wallet and offer cash recompense.

Jettie has been reading this book and offering suggestions for improvement, edit remarks, and making sure I don't write anything that might be construed as offensive. Don't worry, we both know this is a losing battle.

Janet Harriett[46]

I leave the best for last, of course.

To date, Janet's tenure with Apex has been the longest. She worked as my senior editor for nearly five years. Prior to that,

---

[46] I would have remained little more than a quiet Apex fangirl if I hadn't made the best decision of my life one cold, rainy night in an unfamiliar city: I followed three strange men into the basement of a house on a

she provided copy editing services and Apex minion support. These days, she still carries the Apex banner wherever she goes (metaphorically) and assists with the Apex mission when her freelance work and day job allows.

Janet has been great for my public image. Thanks to my deep-in-the-Appalachian accent, many words I say come out sounding profane or nonsensical. "Horror" always came out as "whore." Janet, with a precise speaking style honed from many years of living in the American Midwest and Northwest, is the ideal teacher for pronunciation.

After a few years of being my plus-one and keeping me out of trouble, Justin Stewart realized he was fighting a losing battle and bailed on me. Janet stepped up. She's grabbed my wrist and torn it away from the random cups of blue stuff offered by tall hirsute strangers. She's kept count of my beers, understanding the complex equation of how many it takes to turn me into a drunken asshole. She's beat back my legions of adoring fans with a Billy club she affectionately named "The Widowmaker."

Janet has the patience of a bronze Buddha, and the authority of a prison warden. She's a perfect publishing team member.

---

pitch-black cul-de-sac. Honestly, what could *possibly* go wrong in that scenario? Jason sat on the sofa petting a fluffy white cat like he was Donald Pleasence, while Maurice Broaddus tapped into a bottle of Riesling and Jerry Gordon tried to get me to talk. The first lesson I learned from the three of them: always delegate the hard work to Jerry. Eventually, the guys dragged out of me that I was a copy editor, and Jason let me out of the basement alive in exchange for finishing the copy edits on a zombie novella. Between you and me, I'd never actually read any zombie stories before I agreed to work on *Dead Stay Dead*. **(Janet Harriett)**

For Exposure
Eyewitness Rebuttal
Lesley Conner

First, I think it should be known that in Jason's first draft of chapter 10 he says he'd like to mention some memorable *past* editors, no mention of current. I made a note to him pointing out that some of us are still around and I, for one, have no plans of going anywhere anytime soon. Why would I? I have the best job in the world! I spend my days reading amazing stories, working with the best writers in speculative fiction, and scheming with Jason. And since I work from home, I do it all from the comfort of my couch while wearing my pajamas. Absolutely perfect!

As I'm sure anyone who has done their time minioning for Jason can tell you, being a part of the Apex team is a wonderful way to learn more about publishing, editing, and writing. But there are other truths that I've learned—some about Jason, some about myself—while working for Apex that I wasn't expecting.

1. I'm organized!
looks around at the piles of uncompleted projects, leaning stacks of books, my kids' school papers, and random detritus littering every horizontal surface of my home

Despite the impression I've seemed to have left on Jason, I do not consider myself organized. There are days when finding my car keys is a major accomplishment. But when it comes to Apex, I run a tight ship. While I'm incapable of organizing physical objects, it seems I have a knack for keeping track of files and remembering when projects need to be completed. Sweet!

2. Coffee is serious business. It is also amusing.

Jason takes his coffee seriously. I also take my coffee seriously. Teasing him on Twitter about drinking ALL the coffee and leaving none for him is a highly amusing way to fill those minutes when I'm waiting for the caffeine to kick in. You should try it sometime. His Twitter handle is @apexjason.

3. Jason sometimes draws a blank.

When working with Jason, there will come a time when he will forget absolutely *everything* about something you spoke with him at great lengths about. There's no point in getting irritated. With as many projects as Apex has going on, it is inevitable. Also, see point 4.

4. I sometimes draw a blank, and so will you.

There will come a time when Jason asks you about something and you have no clue what he's going on about because you have completely forgotten about the conversation he swears the two of you had. This has only happened to me a couple of times, but when it has it's been incredibly unsettling. That jarring realization that little pockets of time have been sucked from my life, leaving me with no trace that they had ever been there. *shudder*

This is why I don't get irritated when it happens to Jason. Instead, I recap what we'd already discussed, while wishing that we worked in a normal office setting so I could give him a reassuring pat on the back and a cup of coffee. Surely this is a sign we're both working too hard and coffee fixes everything.

5. Don't ask Jason what project you should work on first!

This one took me a long time to learn. Between *Apex Magazine* and Apex Book Company, we always have multiple projects going on at one time. My to-do list is more like a to-do mountain with random stairways carved into the side, loop-de-loop slides, and doorways that fall into oblivion. Usually I'm on top of it, at the summit if you will, with a running list of what needs to be accomplished first, what can wait till tomorrow, and what may happen in some far off distance that I like to call "When I have time." But occasionally I get overwhelmed and am not sure which way is up. It used to be at times like these I would ask Jason what I should work on first, expecting him to choose one of the many tasks already waiting for me. Instead he would give me a completely new task.

Every. Single. Time.

At first I thought that these new tasks were super important and needed to be put ahead of everything else, so I'd scramble and push and shove my to-do list into shape to somehow get everything done. Then it finally occurred to me that he always gave me some random, out of left field task, and it hit me that he was assuming I was asking because I didn't have anything else waiting for me. That man gives me WAY more credit than he should. So I quit asking.

Now when I'm having an overwhelmed moment, I step away from the computer, make a cup of tea, and take a deep breath. After a few minutes one task always floats to the top of the to-do pile as being the one I should tackle.

6. There are panic, must-be-done-immediately projects.

A couple of years ago at Context I had the pleasure of meeting Maggie Slater. At the time, she was *Apex Magazine*'s interviewer and also put together the eBook files for some of our books. We were sitting at the Apex table, getting to know one another by sharing our Apex experiences. Finally the topic came around to *those* emails. The ones where Jason would ask us to complete some task. Now Jason is constantly dolling out one task or another to me, but these particular emails go something like this:

>Jason: "Can you proofread[47] this book?"

>>Me: "Sure. When do you need it done by?"

>>>Jason: "Yesterday."

>>>>Me: "Um" *shoves everything off my to-do list for the next several days* "Sure, but I'm going to be a bit behind on that deadline."

Maggie and I burst out laughing,[48] startling several people in the dealer's room, because we had both been there, had experienced the same thing, and it was amazing getting to share those experiences with someone we had just met. Between giggles, we decided that these emails must be induced by a deadline sneaking up behind Jason and scaring the snot out of him, at which time he looks around in a panic, then starts emailing people, more or less saying "You, you, and you, create magic!" It feels pretty special to be on Jason's "create magic" email list, even if that specialness comes with a side of "Oh, my! How can I possibly?" panic of my own.

This was the same con that Maggie, Kelly Almond, and I decided heckling your boss during a panel and coming up with an insane rating system with scorecards would be epic! We get along smashingly!

Which brings me to point 7.

7. Working for Apex means making amazing friends!

Being a part of Apex has done so much more than teach me about publishing, or how to be an editor and better writer (and it has certainly done all three of those). I have met some of the most amazing people because of my role with Apex, people who I would call some of my closest friends. I really wish that Maggie, Kelly, and I lived in the same town so we could

---

[47] It doesn't have to be proofreading. It can be some other editing task. (**Lesley Conner**)

[48] I always suspected my super minions laughed at me behind my back. Granted, everything stated here by Lesley is true. (**Jason Sizemore**)

run amok, leaving behind chaos, giggles, and bunny rabbits wherever we went. Jerry Gordon can talk knowledgably on just about any topic, from speakeasies in the 1920s, to home repairs, to industry insights. He is also the best at keeping me on track for my current writing project because while I'm willing to let myself down, he isn't. Andrea Johnson is probably the best human being ever! She is up for any random project I throw her way, and is the type of person who carries blank postcards in her purse so if she does something cool, she can immediately write it down and share it with a friend. And Jason, well, he's one of my best friends. He has seen me at my worst and still seems to believe in me. That is definitely worth something to me.

I can't say for sure why Jason started hiring editors and other minions to help with Apex. Possibly it was to help him reach those 100,000 hours of experience to make him a publishing master, or that his vision of Apex was way larger than what one man could accomplish on his own. What I can say is that what I've gained by being a part of that team is more valuable than an enormous paycheck, tons of prestige, and a fancy award combined. I've learned an immeasurable amount about the career I always wanted but never thought I'd have, and so much more.

8. Truths from Chapter 11

1. I do have a room under my house that looks like a secret government bunker filled with mile after mile of shelving. I keep my books there and hire a maid to dust them. No way I have the time to do it myself!

2. Apparently, I'm not a person. I am a train, or at least the engine, lube, and brake pads parts of a train. Yeah, that's a little weird.

3. I am trying to steal Jason's brain. No, I will not tell you why. That is a secret. But believe me, the end result will be epic!

4. I do in fact get shit done.

Chapter 12: Lord Hugo

I n 2012, seven years of hard work paid off with my first Hugo Award nomination. Our online short fiction publication received a nomination in the category of Best Semiprozine along with other genre luminaries *Locus*, *Lightspeed*, *Interzone*, and *New York Review of Science Fiction*. I never imagined back in 2005 that my little short fiction enterprise would one day be up for the biggest award in science fiction literature.

The Hugo Awards ceremonies are held at WorldCon, the primary professional conference for science fiction, hosted by the World Science Fiction Society. That year, WorldCon was held in Chicago, a mere six-hour drive from Lexington. I decided I would attend.

The last time I had attended a major award ceremony was the 2007 World Horror Con in Toronto when Gill and I were nominated for editing *Aegri Somnia*. With my 2007 experience playing like a soundtrack in my mind, I was a ball of nerves on the drive to Chicago for WorldCon. It was embarrassing to have to run out of the Stoker ceremony. Needing to throw up while in the middle of a large assembly of industry peers is a horrifying experience. The closer I got to Chicago, the more certain I became that it would happen again.

Unlike in Toronto, this time I had Janet Harriett with me. She's a fine person to have around at events like these, particularly if you're anti-social and crippled with anxiety like I am. Janet knows when I need to find a quiet space and recharge. WorldCon, while not the largest of professional conferences, still has 5,000+ attendees. Panel rooms, bars, and walkways get crowded quickly. Having an escort help you fight through the throngs of humanity is a great luxury.

Also, as it turns out, Janet Harriett makes a lovely plus-one for major award banquets.

The day of the Hugo Awards ceremony, I was a complete disaster. Janet made sure I arrived at the awards ceremony walkthrough. She paid attention while the artist showed my fellow nominee John Joseph Adams and I how to wax the rocket (yes, we were tittering like eighth-grade boys) if we got to take one home as winners.

Somehow I had forgotten to pack a T-shirt for my suit and I lacked black socks. Nerves made it impossible for me to knot my tie properly. Janet handled all these problems, no sweat. In the end, I managed a presentable figure in a decent black suit, adorned by my victory goatee (grown special for the occasion) and fashionable pocket square.

Janet, on the other hand, looked like a million dollars. Monica Valentinelli provided an assist with hair and makeup. Janet was decked out in a gorgeous black dress and high heels, and practically glowed. Having her on my arm gave me a +2 bonus to my base charm score.

As instructed, we arrived via a freight elevator that would take the nominees to the awards ceremony. On the walk there, an Apex fan tried to stop me to sign a book, telling me how much he loved the magazine. I did my best to tell him politely I had to go, though I'm not sure it worked. Sorry, guy. I hope you still don't think me rude.

Ninety minutes before the ceremony, all the nominees attended a cocktail mixer. Janet and I walked in and looked around. Everything was lovely and felt very fancy, which only made me twice as nervous. In all my years, I had never attended a cocktail mixer and didn't know what to expect. What I did know was that I would be there rubbing elbows with Neil Gaiman, George R.R. Martin, Seanan McGuire, and many other well-known editors and writers in the science fiction field for more than an hour. The introvert in me wanted to hide. Snacks and drinks were served. I managed to mingle. Some poor soul spilled wine on Mary Robinette Kowal's gorgeous Mae West-style gown (Mary, ever the epitome of grace and manners, took it in stride. She even used an old-fashioned housewife's trick to hide most of the damage.) Although a terrible accident, that spill managed to loosen the nerves of the group of nominees considerably. Even the most famous man in the room, George R.R. Martin, acted nervous.

Finally, an event volunteer called for us to take our seats at the front of the ballroom at the foot of the stage. A table of Hugo rockets sparkled under the stage lights, beckoning us. Until that moment when I saw the table of trophies I had no idea just how badly I wanted to win. The urge subsumed me.

Janet leaned in and said something.

"What?" I shook off the reverie.

"Do you have an acceptance speech ready? You know, for when you win."

Dammit!

I had a speech ready, but of course I'd left it in the hotel room.

Janet read my stricken face. "Quick, write something up on your phone."

There wasn't time to throw anything formal together. Instead I built a list of names I didn't want to forget when giving thanks.

The ballroom lights darkened, and the evening's host, John Scalzi, appeared. The show was on.

The categories and winning speeches crept by. I mumbled "Get to it, already" over and over to myself. I'm pretty sure Janet would have shot me with a tranquilizer gun if she'd had one on hand. Sweat practically dripped from my hands and forehead.

Finally, finally, Scalzi announced that the next award to be given out was for Best Semiprozine. My editor-in-chief, Lynne M. Thomas, sitting a row ahead of me, reached back and took my hand. She smiled in a reassuring manner.

And the winner of the Hugo Award for Best Semiprozine goes to Locus Magazine.

My conscience took a dive into a dark place. I'd never felt so disappointed in my whole life.

All smiles because I had
yet to lose.

One great thing about the Hugo Award event is the Hugo Losers Party after it's over. The losers were shuttled in the freight elevator to a large suite outfitted with snacks, drinks, and food shaped like Hugo trophies. We got to mingle and wallow in our failures.

The party quickly became crowded. My reserves of social stamina emptied after an hour, so Janet ushered me out of the party and back to my hotel room. We grabbed some real food, went to the lounge/bar area for a while to hang out, and I finally called it a night around 2 a.m.

I'm waiting for one of the eight elevators to open and shuttle me back to my nest when somebody taps me on my shoulder. I turn.

Oh no. Hickory Adams.

I sighed. "Hello, Mr. Adams."

"Mr. Sizemore, I did not vote for *Apex Magazine* to win."

"That's okay. One vote wouldn't have made a difference."

"Two votes. I bought a voting membership for my wife. Two votes cast against you."

Hickory's rheumy eyes glared at me.

"Let's get this over worth. Do you have anything to pitch?"

"I'd like to pitch you into Lake Michigan."

That one made me smile. "Goodnight, Hickory," I said. The elevator in front of me opened. I stepped inside.

"That's Mr. Adams to you, you liberal asshole!"

The doors shut.

Since the 2007 Toronto hotel incident, I typically get a private room at conventions. Since WorldCon is more expensive than the small fandom events I often attend, I roomed with Maurice Broaddus so we could split the cost.

That was a mistake.

As I seem to do a lot, I fell asleep on my bed face-first. This is unfortunate. Through years of study, I've determined that the face-first position is best way to drool all over yourself. On this night, I had been playing with my iPhone in the dark, in my boxers, unwinding, before I dozed off. Then at some point in the night, my roommate, Maurice Broaddus, appeared with a group of female writer friends to pick up copies of his new book. They all poured inside. He switched on the light.

"What the—" I mumbled.

Laughter. Lots of laughter. I clumsily threw a pillow over my booty and missed.

My trip back to Lexington was uneventful. I didn't even come down with any unusual and cruelly painful health problems. I did get in trouble the following Tuesday on my return to the day job and was nearly written up. A middle manager felt like he needed something finished while I was gone and expressed his unhappiness to my boss. I didn't care. I'd had an incredible weekend with friends and colleagues. I enjoyed every minute of WorldCon. Over the course of seven years, I had worked thousands of hours and it had paid off with a nomination for the field's highest honor.

I am the first ever Hugo Award nominee from the community of Big Creek, Kentucky.

I am the first ever Hugo Award nominee from Clay County, one of the country's poorest areas, nestled deep in the hills of Appalachia.

People I know back in the hills love to remind me of these two facts. I'm proud to have done something worth their admiration.

In 2005, I had an early midlife crisis and decided I wanted to leave a positive mark on the world. Apex Publications has allowed me to do that. When I reflect on the successes my past and current editors, writers, and artists have enjoyed, I can't help but smile. If I played a role in helping any single one of these wonderful, creative people achieve their dreams of bringing their talents to bear for the masses, I'll feel like I've accomplished something important.[49]

I can't wait to see what the next ten years of Apex has in store for me....

---

[49] Apex is always going to do well, no matter what changes occur in publishing. Rise of the eBooks. A torrent of self-published authors. Shitty economy. No matter. Jason is willing to put in the hard work and sacrifice needed to make sure Apex succeeds. He'll sacrifice his time, sanity, friendships he's had since high school, the tires on his car, reams of paper, chickens, the occasional goat. Hell, do you have a virgin? I'm sure he could find the appropriate chants and rituals to appease the gods and make sure Apex continues to thrive. It's dirty, bloody work, but he's willing to do it. **(Lesley Conner)**

Lord Hugo
Eyewitness Rebuttal

Janet Harriet

Before we get into the meat of rebutting Jason's memories of losing his first Hugo, I would like to take a moment to properly thank Monica Valentinelli for her hard work in making me look, as Jason so kindly put it, "like a million dollars" for Hugo Night 2012. Not only did Monica work fashion magic with someone whose idea of "doing my hair" was breaking out the fancy ponytail holder, but she did it with grace even after the incident alluded to in Footnote 37 (about which I will not go into in detail, because what is this, a tell-all memoir of Apex's first decade or something?). For what it's worth, my money is on Monica to win the cage match that will decide Jason's plus-one for his fourth Hugo Award nomination.

That said....

By the 2012 WorldCon, I'd been Jason's convention buddy enough times to get his con rhythms down and develop several responses to people who mistook me for his wife. WorldCon as a Hugo nominee was a whole new level. Jason was trying to cram four years of business into four days, all while staffing a vendor table, getting an issue of *Apex Magazine* ready to go out to subscribers the day after the convention,[50] and attending to all of the pomp that comes with being a Hugo nominee. My role became less "remind him not to eat the ham" and more "remind him to eat something at all." Don't drink the blue stuff, and whatever you drink, go to the restroom *before* sitting on the 90-minute panel.

Jason had already taken half a day out of taking care of Apex business to prepare for the Hugo ceremony. Part of the

---

[50] Magazine publication schedules are harsh mistresses, and they do not care that the weekend usually reserved for magazine pre-release work is also the weekend celebrating the editors' accomplishments with said magazine **(Janet Harriett)**

preparation, I swear on my March 1967 *IF* magazine, really did involve learning how to clean a Hugo Award with a bottle of lemon Pledge (let me tell you, the inevitable rocket-waxing jokes never stop being funny). There was a cocktail reception that, judging by the previous chapter, Jason recalls only slightly better than the night he agreed to publish *Dark Faith*. Since I was not the nominee, I have vague recollections of appetizers, getting bumped into by George R.R. Martin, and a delightful conversation with Christie Yant and John Joseph Adams before we got herded into the room where some of us would become Hugo Award winners.

Having watched awards shows on TV, I always assumed that beat between "And the winner is...." and announcing the winner was to build tension for the audience. After sitting next to Jason during his first Hugo Awards ceremony as a nominee, I now know that the beat is so the nominees can savor the last crumb of possibility. In that beat exists the chance to be a winner. The next breath out of the presenter's mouth collapses the probability wave, creating losers. However, for one final, delightful moment, everyone still has hope.

But let me take you back to fifteen minutes before Jason lost his first Hugo. Be a fly on my shoulder, and see with me the should-be-iconic image of a small press. We're packed as tight as fire codes will allow in the second row of Hugo nominees. People around us are dressed to the nines to celebrate the accomplishments of an industry that, if social media and Lesley Conner's rebuttal are to be believed, rarely wears pants of the non-pajama variety. Jason is wearing a fancy new suit, and, in lieu of the forgotten undershirt, an inside-out white T-shirt with that Groucho Marx quote about reading inside a dog. The gleaming tower of Hugo Awards on their frosted-glass bases shrinks as the probability wave collapses for more and more people around us. Some guy behind us (whom I later learn is Christopher J. Garcia) leaps up and hugs every winner as they make their way to the steps to claim their rockets and make their thank-yous. Even though the stage blazes with lights, it's dark in our row of nominees... except for a faint glow coming from my left.

Jason is tapping out an acceptance speech on his iPhone.

That image, for me, captures the spirit of Apex.

I'd been pestering him for weeks to get an acceptance speech sketched out, just in case. He always had more pressing things to attend to than prepare for such a long shot. At last, in the middle of the ceremony, it hit him that there was a chance of success. And if there was a chance of success, he would prepare for it. *Apex Magazine* came in second that year, but as we waited for the probability wave to collapse around us, Jason still dared hope things would go his way, and he would be ready.

Prognosticating the future is no easy feat. I have a general idea of where I see Apex Publications and myself in ten years. The vision consists of great sums of money, fame, and adoration. Because describing my utopia would be boring, I decided to ask a group of intelligent and wise individuals the following question:

How do you see Apex Publications and/or
Jason Sizemore in ten years?

These are the answers I received.

Parting Shot
"Faithful Reader"

Jettie Necole, Apex Director of Quality Assurance

See the man holding the remote control, eyeing the device with a heavy tap of his curled finger. That's Jason Sizemore. He's finally done it! Taken over the world. *Apex Science Fiction and Horror Digest* was the beginning of the end. For humanity that is....

♦

If I had more time or word count requirements, I'd share the story of how *Apex Magazine* reached 98.9% of the science fiction community. How Sizemore's bank account grew to such epic proportions he funded the first society on the moon, where baby Jasons and Jasonannas were born into Apex Nation. After the Apex Revolution, 59% of the new male population was named Jason. Ever meet a Jesus? Same concept when you meet a Jason, a truly religious experience. I could tell you about the time his first novel hit the bestseller list, causing the largest human trampling to occur at its release! Don't get me started on the tattoos created from such pandemonium that rival the tramp stamp, now referred to as trampled stamp.

Instead, I'll share the story of the faithful reader. Another double-X-chromosome individual overcome by Sizemore's first superpower. A young girl with an impressionable mind, who'd one day use Sizemore's life's work to build the future. An intellect so high it would tip the scales of technological evolution and bring about the end of days for primitive thinking. The advancement of technology being her avenue for not saying sorry for her irredeemable path. No regrets, using brother Sizemore, wait....

Did I mention he also delivers sermons to ready and willing minds at the Sacrament of Sizemore? Well, guess I just did.

Brother Sizemore has also taken a stance on the Sizemore Standards of Living, five impactful truths to living your life to the fullest.

You want to know what the five steps are? Well, I'm scared to share. It could disrupt the future timeline and cause a parallel breach that might destroy everything. Instead, I'll stick to the safe points. Those five standards are simply brilliant and one day, you'll see.

Back to the young girl, we'll call her the prodigy of Sizemore for safety. The John Connor thing is a possibility. I don't believe Sizemore truly realized his ability of reaching young minds, but he excelled with this group. Documentation shows Sizemore saw youth, teenagers, to be more specific, as scary. Though, wouldn't you know it, young adults are what brought him his billions and greatest of successes.

The prodigy of Sizemore first received *Apex Magazine* at the age of ten, growing up with Apex, cultivating her young mind, feeding her creative psyche. The greatest inventor to grace the human race greedily ate up every story published by Sizemore. Impatiently waiting for what came next, like an addict shooting up with Lou Reed singing "Heroin", Apex Publications was her oasis. Words can change a person. They can motivate. They bring rise to new opinions, new ways of living, new ways of thinking. They can also create faith. For our prodigy, it was the latter. She believed technology was faith.

World War III would be fought and won by her creation, Templar 3, the third generation in robotic super intelligence. Her nod to Sizemore's own early works in "Mr. Templar," where an android is lost in a wasteland as his energy depletes. The idea never left her and with it sparked the conception of artificial intelligence, reaching the level of world domination. Once they surpassed all capacity for what their programming managed, they became self-aware.

The rest is history. The end was swift and humanity was surprised. It did hurt. I won't say it didn't.

Not to say a few Jasons didn't survive. It's a possibility. Highly unlikely, but I imagine sometimes, a few can still be found floating on the moon.

👾

See Sizemore, holding the remote, tapping at it with a disagreeable and elderly grumble. Before him stands an android of superior design. A wooden crate sits next to it, open, with a note resting atop. Written in print it says:

> *Dear Mr. Sizemore,*
> *Enjoy my Mr. Templar,[51] first model off the assembly line. I have created him in your likeness. A token of all my admiration and appreciation for your words and the words you advocate for others.*
> *Your faithful reader*

👾

Or I could tell you about the time Jason Sizemore woke up and realized it was all a dream....

---

[51] Mr. Templar is the beloved protagonist of my most popular short story, "Mr. Templar." You should read it sometime in my collection *Irredeemable*. (**Jason Sizemore**)

Parting Shot
"Unless..."

Maggie Slater, Apex Publications Assistant Editor

W hen I joined *Apex Magazine* (*Apex Science Fiction and Horror Digest*, at the time) some seven years ago, I had *no idea* how big it would get by 2015. I mean, we were tiny back then—just five or six people doing all the slushing, all the marketing, all the promoting, and editing—and just look at how far Apex has come! Multiple Hugo nominations for the magazine, a couple Stoker Awards for our authors, a major fan base, and a whole army of minions working tirelessly behind the scenes. I mean, Jason's been on panels with *John Joseph Adams* multiple times! He's that big now!

And all of that in the ten years since Jason brought Apex to life. I mean, what could possibly happen in the next ten years to rival that? I mean....

...unless Jason's secretly a serial killer... (See 1)
...unless aliens are reading *Apex Magazine*... (See 2)

1

But what if Jason's just been using Apex's dark fiction as a cover for his serial killing? It gives him the perfect excuse to talk about disemboweling people, babies drinking blood, and evil clowns from space. If he suddenly confessed to killing fourteen or fifteen people over the course of the next ten years, you think anyone would even believe him? No way! Someone would just laugh, get him another drink, and try pitching him a brand new *Twilight*-Meets-*Tremors* novel. Which of course, would end up leading to victim #16, so mutilated that the cops will have to whip out those old dental records to ID. And Jason'll get away with it, too...

...unless an Apex editor catches him in the act... (See 3)
...unless the convention hotel sits on a toxic landfill...(See 5)

2

What if aliens have been reading *Apex Magazine* for years and finally decide to attend a convention just to meet Jason, Mr. Head Bossborg himself, in person. Maybe one of the aliens even has a novel it's hoping to pitch to Jason that it really, really, *really* thinks is going to just blow the heads off the Earthling readership. And you know what? After a couple of shots of some strange alien booze, Jason might just say, "Yeah, okay! Let's try it." So he publishes this alien text — translated, of course, with two volumes of footnotes to explain it to humans, which *I'll* probably have to format... — and it becomes this *huge* best seller! It wins every award, including the Nobel Prize, and humanity unites within the fandoms that blossom from this book...

...unless a big publisher gets jealous...(See 4)
...unless the alien author is a plagiarist...(See 6)

3

Until some hapless Apex editor or intern happens to witness the brutal execution. Whoever it is — we'll say it's a she, because most of Jason's editors are ladies — will stumble back from the blood-splattered green room where Jason had lured Victim 16, before stabbing them to death with an Apex-branded pen. Jason will beg her not to tell, to just keep this one dark little secret for him — I mean, they're friends, aren't they? And anyways, he'd never hurt *her* — and she'll think about it, but eventually swear to silence...

...unless she's an FBI agent... (See 7)
...unless she's a serial killer, too... (See 11)

4

Of course, the editor-in-chief of some big publishing house (or maybe CEO of an online retailer...) — driven mad by the unimaginable success of a small press and the inevitable crumbling of traditional publishing houses — decides to ruin everything. After all, if one book is all Earth needs to be completely fulfilled, the book industry will be on the brink of collapse! This individual will organize a plot to kidnap the alien author in order to force it to write a twelve-book series — with an exclusive contract! — and no one will be able to stop it...

...unless Jason finds out... (See 9)
...unless the plan goes wrong... (See 13)

5

But like most convention hotels, this one was built over a toxic landfill, and when he buries Victim 16 beneath one of the sculpted shrubberies beside the Emergency Exit door, the toxic fluids seep into the corpse, reanimating it. When it crawls its way out of the ground and stumbles into the dealer's room, everyone laughs and starts forming a zombie-walk behind it. That is, until Victim 16 whips around and noshes on one of the con-goer's brains. Then all hell breaks loose, and the zombie apocalypse will be upon us!

Unless Jason realizes what's happening... (See 8)
Unless this was Jason's plan all along... (See 12)

6

Oops. Turns out the alien author stole every word and symbol of its book from another of its species, and *that* alien happens to be a pretty powerful general in the alien army. Of course, it's not going to sit on its multiple-rears and let this stand! So it calls in the entire alien armada and demands that Earth burn or delete every copy of the imposter's book, or face planetary extinction. Earth's governments scramble to determine if they have enough military strength to defeat an alien onslaught, but it's not looking too good. And that'll be it...

...unless Jason listens to another alien book pitch...(See 10)
...unless Jason turns over the traitorous alien author...(See 14)

7

Unless she's actually an FBI agent and has secretly been tracking the Book-Pitch Basher. When Jason tries to flee, she tackles him to the ground and a SWAT team rushes in to arrest him, while the con-goers look on in shock, glad *they* didn't pitch a stupid book idea. It'll be a *Locus* cover story, and Jason'll go on trial, and probably get the death penalty, unless... **(See End)**

8

A quick glance tells Jason what's happened. He grabs a copy of Apex's heaviest book—probably *I Remember the Future*—and starts whaling wholesale on Victim 16 until its head bashes in and it drops. Others in the dealer's room will cheer and join in, taking out the infected zombie walkers. And Jason will be given a new Hugo Award for *Best-Zombie Slaying*, unless... **(See End)**

9

Through his minion spy network, Jason gets wind of this evil plot, and assembles a crack-team of down-and-out authors and scientists to stop it. Little did anybody know, but Jason's been working on building a top-secret spaceship in all that free time he has. Together with his rag-tag team, he intercepts the evil CEO's henchmen just as they're escaping with the alien author, and the world will rejoice unless... **(See End)**

10

The only thing that will appease the General, other than total global annihilation, is for Jason to listen to its book pitch of a *different* novel. Fearfully, Jason agrees, and—what do you know!—the book sounds amazing! At least as good as, if not better than, the stolen one. And Jason realizes he's got the universe's best author begging to publish with Apex! Of course, he signs the General to a contract, and makes a bazillion dollars, unless... **(See End)**

11

Of course, being an Apex minion makes for just about as good a cover as being editor-in-chief. The editor, a serial killer herself, realizes that she can pin all of her previous murders on Jason, *and* take over the company. So she promises secrecy, and—more importantly—sympathy, which of course Jason desperately needs, since he never meant to start killing would-be writers. And when she knows all his secrets, she'll kill him and frame him, and no one will know, unless... **(See End)**

12

As the zombies flood the convention, Jason slips out a side door, his glasses flashing in that oh-so-sinister way. Of course, this was Jason's plan all along. People thought zombie fiction had run its course? THE FOOLS! As the zombie infestation sweeps the nation, and then the world, Jason starts his own cult on the basis of his prophetic publishing of zombie fiction and brilliant survival strategies. He'll soon become the adored leader of the uninfected, chief of The Cult of Apex, unless... **(See End)**

13

But the alien is killed by accident when they kidnap it! With its author martyred, the book becomes even more popular. But the alien author was a royal personage, and its death enrages its people. They send a massive armada of ships to Earth. In the face of extinction, Jason hunts down the evil CEO, they duke it out on top of the Burj Khalifa in Dubai, appeasing the alien invaders' bloodlust, unless... **(See End)**

14

Jason must turn over the traitor within forty-eight hours. It's then that a coalition of world secret agencies approaches him with a plan: deliver the traitor to the enemy, and sneak a device on board that will destroy the mothership from the inside. Of course, Jason alerts the invaders of this plan, and in thanks they blow up Earth but let him come with them back to their planet. Unless... **(See End)**

END

...this is all ridiculous nonsense, and no one knows where Apex and Jason will be in the next ten years...but it's bound to be better than any of that!

Parting Shot

"I Remember the Future of Apex Publications"

Michael A. Burstein, author of *I Remember the Future* (Apex Publications, 2008)

As soon as the time cabinet materialized in the year 2015, I jumped out to find Jason Sizemore. Fortunately, the Spatio-Temporal Positioning System was working perfectly. He was in the bathroom of Joseph-Beth Booksellers in Lexington, Kentucky, taking a break from mingling with the huge crowd that had come to attend the Apex Tenth Anniversary Bash. I knocked on the door of his stall.

"Jason, it's Michael Burstein," I said. "I have come... from the future!"

He flushed the toilet and emerged. "Let me just wash my hands," he said.

After he finished, he turned to me. "So you got my note?"

"I did indeed. I'm here to tell you what happens to Apex Publications over the next decade," I said.

"Well?" he asked, raising his chin slightly.

"Well," I echoed, "it's not a pretty picture." And with that, I told him all about the bankruptcy that had destroyed Apex because of the Great Fiction Implosion of 2020.

"Alas," he said. "What can we do to prevent it?"

"Hand the company over to my current self," I replied. "After all, I have ten Hugo nominations and four Nebula nominations. Surely my earlier self will be able to figure out a way out of this mess."

"Indeed!" Jason replied. He quickly grabbed a few squares of toilet paper and we wrote out a contract assigning Apex over to me.

Jason shook my hand. "Good luck to both of us," he said, and he scurried out of the bathroom.

As soon as he was gone, I released an evil chuckle.

My plan had worked perfectly.

When I got back to the future, the multibillion dollar Apex Publishing Company would be mine.[52]

---

[52] Poor deluded Michael. If there's any lesson to be taken away from this book, it is that you'll have to pry Apex out of my cold, dead hands! **(Jason Sizemore)**

Parting Shot

"Feeding the Beast"

Jaym Gates, Co-Editor of *War Stories*
(Apex Publications, 2014)

Jason Sizemore in ten years? Crazy cat lady, obviously, surrounded by tons of books and cats and cat-books and book-cats (look, if you think *I'm* making this up, go watch *Mirrormask*) and authors, and cats who are authors. He'll get up in the morning to feed everyone, and by the time he's done, it will be time to feed everyone again.

But it's fine, because he's a publisher, and everyone knows that publishers don't sleep, and subsist on the blood of their authors.

Better sign some more talent, Jason; the current crop is starting to look a little anemic.[53]

---

[53] Obviously, Jaym's prediction is the one you should bet on. **(Jason Sizemore)**

Acknowledgements

Running a small business requires countless sacrifices and many levels of support from those you love. I thank my wife Susan and the kids (Lindsey and Ryan) for their patience and understanding as I spend ridiculous amounts of time locked away in my office publishing books and magazines.

So many people have donated their time and energy to Apex over the years that I could fill half the books with names. None of this would exist without: Justin Stewart, Deb Taber, Gill Ainsworth, Maggie Slater, Lesley Conner, Janet Harriett, Sarah E. Olsen, Maurice Broaddus, McKenzie Johnston-Winberry, Jerry Gordon, Elaine Blose, Geoffrey Girard, Alethea Kontis, Lavie Tidhar, MG Ellington, Jettie Necole, DeAnna Knippling, Steph Jacob, Athena Workman, Hannah Krieger, and Monica Valentinelli.

Finally, thank you to the fans of Apex Publications and my writing!

About the Author

Born the son of an unemployed coal miner in a tiny Kentucky Appalachian villa named Big Creek (population 400), Jason fought his way out of the hills to the big city of Lexington. He attended Transylvania University (a real school with its own vampire legend) and received a degree in computer science. Since 2005, he has owned and operated Apex Publications. He is the editor of five anthologies, author of *Irredeemable*, a three-time Hugo Award loser, and occasional writer, who can usually be found wandering the halls of hotel conventions seeking friends and free food.

About the Contributors

Elaine Blose is a writer who lives with a three pound rabbit who thinks he's a ninja and that bunnies living in the wild is a complete myth. Her work has appeared in *Dark Futures* and *The Zombie Feed: Volume 1*.

Maurice Broaddus is the coeditor of *Dark Faith* and *Streets of Shadows*. His Knights of Breton Court urban fantasy series was recently released by Angry Robot. *Walkers with the Dawn*, Maurice's new collection of short fiction, is now available. Learn more at MauriceBroaddus.com.

Michael A. Burstein is the award-winning author of *I Remember the Future*. He lives in Brookline, Massachusetts, with his wife and twin daughters. Visit his website at www.mabfan.com.

Lesley Conner is the managing editor of Apex Publications and the author of *The Weight of Chains*, an alternative history horror novel coming out through Sinister Grin Press in 2015. To find out more, follow her on Twitter at @LesleyConner.

Jaym Gates is an editor (*War Stories: New Tales of Military SF*), author, and communications director who spends all her time trying to figure out how to use fewer words. You can find more information at jaymgates.com.

Geoffrey Girard hates writing and is a Stoker-nominated author of dark fiction and YA novels. Find out more at www.GeoffreyGirard.com.

Janet Harriett is the senior editor for Apex Publications. Her fiction has appeared in *Not Our Kind* and *Ravenwood: Stepson of Mystery, Volume 2*. Find her online at www.JanetHarriett.com and @janetharriett.

Sara M. Harvey lives and writes fantasy and horror in (and sometimes about) Nashville, TN. She tweets @saraphina_marie, wastes too much time on facebook.com/saramharvey, and needs to update her website saramharvey.com.

Jettie Necole is the Kentucky born author of *The Vault* and Tree of Blood series. She holds a degree in Film and Television from the University of Texas at Austin. Visit her at www.jettienecole.com.

Justin Stewart is informed in all facets of art and design. He's been working for Apex since the beginning of the company, doing book design and various other artwork. Justin's also done work for Disney, Marvel Comics, Image Comics, Archaia, Boom! Studios, Viper Comics, and Zenoscope Studios. Find Justin on Twitter @Justin3000 or visit his site at www.Justin3000.com.

Maggie Slater writes and shivers in the still-icy shadows of New England's old-growth forests. Her fiction has appeared in *Dark Futures: Tales of SF Dystopia, Leading Edge Magazine,* and most recently in *Zombies: More Recent Dead* from Prime Books. Visit her online at maggiedot.wordpress.com.

Monica Valentinelli is a writer and editor who lurks in the dark. Visit her website at www.mlvwrites.com. She is coediting with Jaym Gates the upcoming Apex Publications anthology *Upside Down: Inverted Tropes in Storytelling.*

APEX PUBLICATIONS NEWSLETTER

Why sign up?

Newsletter-only promotions. Book release announcements. Event invitations. And much, much more!

Subscribe and receive a **15%** discount code for your next order from ApexBookCompany.com!

If you choose to sign up for the Apex Publications newsletter, we will send you an email confirmation to insure that you in fact requested the newsletter and to avoid unwanted emails. Your email address is always kept confidential, and we will only use it to send you newsletters or special announcements. You may unsubscribe at any time, and details on how to unsubscribe are included in every newsletter email.

Visit
HTTP://WWW.APEXBOOKCOMPANY.COM/PAGES/NEWSLETTER

SING ME YOUR SCARS

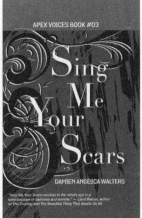

APEX VOICES BOOK #03

In her first collection of short fiction, Damien Walters weaves her lyrical voice through suffering and sorrow, teasing out the truth and discovering hope.

BY DAMIEN ANGELICA WALTERS

"*Sing Me Your Scars* revolves in the mind's eye in a kaleidoscope of darkness and wonder."
Laird Barron, author of *The Croning* and *The Beautiful Thing That Awaits Us All*

"Anatomies of dreams and nightmares, Walters is a writer to watch."
John Langan, author of *The Wide, Carnivorous Sky and Other Monstrous Geographies*

ISBN: 978-1-937009-28-1 ~ ApexBookCompany.com